CW01183585

KYOTOFU

KYOTOFU

UNIQUELY DELICIOUS JAPANESE DESSERTS

NICOLE BERMENSOLO
with ELIZABETH GUNNISON DUNN

RUNNING PRESS
PHILADELPHIA · LONDON

© 2015 by Nicole Bermensolo
Photographs © 2015 by Steve Legato
Photographs © 2015 on pages 12 and 13, by Jerry Erico
Published by Running Press,
A Member of the Perseus Books Group

All rights reserved under the Pan-American and
International Copyright Conventions

Printed in China

This book may not be reproduced in whole or in part, in any form or by any means, electronic or mechanical, including photocopying, recording, or by any information storage and retrieval system now known or hereafter invented, without written permission from the publisher.

Books published by Running Press are available at special discounts for bulk purchases in the United States by corporations, institutions, and other organizations. For more information, please contact the Special Markets Department at the Perseus Books Group, 2300 Chestnut Street, Suite 200, Philadelphia, PA 19103, or call (800) 810-4145, ext. 5000, or e-mail special.markets@perseusbooks.com.

ISBN 978-0-7624-5397-9
Library of Congress Control Number: 2014948620

E-book ISBN 978-0-7624-5602-4

9 8 7 6 5 4 3 2 1
Digit on the right indicates the number of this printing

Design by Susan Van Horn
Edited by Zachary Leibman
Typography: Neutra and Mr. Eaves

Running Press Book Publishers
2300 Chestnut Street
Philadelphia, PA 19103-4371

Visit us on the web!
www.offthemenublog.com

捧
呈

This book is dedicated to my family,
who has tirelessly supported me through the Kyotofu journey.

contents

9 INTRODUCTION
20 STOCKING A JAPANESE PANTRY
25 SOURCES
26 A NOTE ON GLUTEN-FREE & VEGAN DESSERTS

大豆
SOY
頁 28

味噌
MISO
頁 52

緑茶
GREEN TEA
頁 68

胡麻
SESAME
頁
94

米
RICE
頁
116

ゆず
YUZU
頁
132

154   BASICS & ACCOMPANIMENTS
172   ACKNOWLEDGMENTS
173   INDEX

本 KYOTOFU

INTRODUCTION

THE IDEA FOR KYOTOFU first came to me in 2005, as I was standing with a spoon hanging out of my mouth on the production floor of a fourth generation tofu factory in Kyoto, Japan. Surrounded by ancient wooden tofu presses and sturdy, spotless vats of warming soy milk, I dug a fresh spoon deep into a just-set batch of silken tofu and rolled the warm, velvety custard around on my tongue, pulling the kinds of faces that tend to make modest Japanese hosts really uncomfortable.

This tofu! Seriously: This. Tofu. My overwhelming urge was to gather it up in my arms, wrap it around myself like a blanket, and bring it back with me to New York. Not just the tofu, which I knew would be a revelation to anyone who has formed their opinions of that word from the packaged stuff languishing in supermarket refrigerator cases—but the whole Japanese approach to eating. From that day, I've been a big believer that Japan's cultural obsession with high-quality food is one of the main reasons that its people live longer and stay healthier than anyone else on earth.

I have always had a thing for Japan. Growing up in New Jersey, I watched the original *Iron Chef* while my friends watched *Beverly Hills, 90210*. While they read Sweet Valley High books, I read manga comics. I was without a doubt the only little Italian girl on the Jersey Shore begging her mother to go to the Japanese bookstore in Manhattan. My freshman year of college, I began studying the language and as a sophomore, I won a scholarship from the Japanese government to study in Japan. Once I got there, it took my friends and family two years to get me back to America.

My studies were based in Tokyo, but it was Kyoto—the country's historical capital, a couple hours away by high speed bullet train—that really captured my imagination and won my heart.

Balance is a guiding principle in Japanese lives, and one that's particularly well represented in their meals.

Where Tokyo is fast-paced and modern, Kyoto is slow and traditional, the kind of city that begs to be explored by bicycle. Tokyo may be the twenty-first century seat of commerce and government, but Kyoto remains the true cultural and food capital of Japan. It's filled with traditional architecture (unlike Tokyo, Kyoto was spared from bombing in World War II), and is home to a staggering 2,000 temples and shrines. It's also famous for its long-standing artisan culture. Here you'll find some of Japan's best and most traditional kimono makers, woodworkers, and of course, small family tofu factories and other food businesses. Kyoto charmed me from my first visit and whenever I return to Japan, I always return to Kyoto.

My relationship with the place took a turn once I left school and entered the working world, embarking on the kind of career where I found myself eating all my meals out of cardboard takeout containers and getting a larger portion of my sleep than I'd care to admit in the back of taxi cabs or curled up in a ball in my desk chair. Revisiting Japan at this point in my life was a wake-up call. It became clear what I was drawn to in this culture, and how painfully far from it my life had strayed.

I'm talking, for starters, about balance. It's a guiding principle in Japanese lives, and one that's particularly well represented in their meals. A typical Japanese breakfast consists of fish and miso soup for protein, pickles for vegetables, and rice for starch: every food group, flavor, and texture in harmony. In a traditional tea ceremony, you drink bitter matcha alongside a dainty Japanese tea sweet: bitter and sweet in balance. The Western concept of binge and fast, boom and bust, indulge and economize—it just makes no sense to the Japanese.

The beauty of the Japanese approach to eating—and living—goes far deeper. Take the simplicity of Japanese aesthetics, which in light of the overscheduled, overstuffed, over-the-top Manhattan world that I inhabited suddenly felt like a cool drink of water. For the first time I really saw Ryoan-ji, the Zen temple in Kyoto, for its clean lines and structural honesty. I saw the poignancy in humble dishes: a sliver of eel on rice; miso paste dissolved in dashi broth; foods that offered pure, clean, simple flavors.

Where in Western culture we place great emphasis on growing our businesses, our fortunes, our homes, our lives, in Japan success is all about achieving mastery of one, small domain. There are entire businesses that make only *kuromitsu* syrup, only matcha tea powder, only a specific type of rice cracker, and have done so for gen-

Eating is always a dedicated activity, aimed at deriving maximum pleasure from a diminutive portion.

erations. The astounding pride taken in one's work product means that there isn't much in the way of low-quality, throwaway food to be found in Japan. For the most part, a person's honor is tied up in the quality of the food he or she makes.

Then there's the sense of slow deliberateness with which good food is to be enjoyed. Japanese children are taught to "eat with their eyes first" and to stop, savor, and respect the beauty of the dish. A Japanese dessert may only be a few bites, but the eater approaches them mindfully and reverently. You don't see people in Japan eating on the street, in the subway, or in their cars. Eating is always a dedicated activity, aimed at deriving maximum pleasure from a diminutive portion.

本
KYOTOFU

Kyotofu Dessert Bar, 2006

    When in 2006 my friend Michael and I opened Kyotofu in the Hell's Kitchen neighborhood of Manhattan, we were taking an enormous leap of faith. My approach to Japanese desserts isn't a conventional one, and it involves a healthy amount of rule breaking. Without getting too technical: Traditional Japanese sweets are called *wagashi*, and they are like edible, miniature pieces of art, intended to be given as gifts rather than eaten as a part of everyday life (much in the same way we treat boxed chocolates in America). But Japan has had a love affair with Western-style sweets ever since Commodore Perry opened the country to foreign trade in the 1850s. To the Japanese, these two categories are very separate: *Wagashi* are made from traditional Japanese ingredients according to age-old methods, and Western sweets like strawberry shortcake, cheesecake, and French pâtisserie are made in more-or-less the Western ways. Food and ingredient conventions for the most part are immutable.

My approach to Japanese desserts isn't a conventional one, and it involves a healthy amount of rule breaking.

Tofu, for instance, is nothing other than a savory dish to the Japanese. Maybe only an Italian American, raised on unctuous crème caramel, panna cotta, luscious mascarpone cream, and *budino* pudding would make any connection at all between dessert and the unbelievable silken product traditionally made by Kyoto's artisans.

本
KYOTOFU

頁
14

Or add miso, the umami-boosting fermented rice and soybean paste, to amplify and deepen the chocolaty richness of brownies.

Or flavor sweet, creamy cheesecake with matcha, the bitter, earthy green tea powder.

Or incorporate kinako, the roasted soybean flour, to add a toasty flavor and rustic texture to shortbread.

We spent seven incredible years running Kyotofu as a full-service restaurant and bakery, gaining a solid group of neighborhood regulars and garnering praise from some of the city's toughest critics.

Manhattan turned out to be a tremendously receptive audience for my quirky approach to Japanese sweets. We spent seven incredible years running Kyotofu as a full-service restaurant and bakery, gaining a solid group of neighborhood regulars and garnering praise from some of the city's toughest critics. By 2013, we were ready for the next step. While Kyotofu had always sold baked goods—cupcakes, shortbread, muffins, and the like—from the front of our restaurant and through a handful of retailers like Dean & Deluca and Williams Sonoma, I had come to realize that it was the bakery, not the sit-down restaurant, which really interested me. Whole Foods had expressed an interest in carrying our products—a partnership which would provide an incredible platform for sharing my desserts on a whole new scale. At the same time, Michael was ready to move on to the next chapter in his life. We decided to shutter the restaurant so I could focus my full attention on building Kyotofu into a bigger, better bakery business.

One of the first things I needed was a commercial kitchen to bake in. I was lucky to be connected through a mutual friend with Chef Mike Hsu, a skilled pastry chef with a background in five-star hotel kitchens who owned a 12,000 square foot commercial kitchen space on the Brooklyn waterfront; he rented the space out to a rotating group of small food businesses in need of part-time kitchen space. At first, Kyotofu became his largest tenant, renting half the facility seven days a week. We soon realized how much we could offer each other: Mike's deep pastry knowledge would be a huge asset to Kyotofu, and my management background would make a big impact on his budding food business incubator. So we became partners in Hana Kitchens, which today makes all of Kyotofu's sweets and rents kitchen space to small, artisan food producers. In addition to our Brooklyn kitchen, we now run a second space of the same size in Los Angeles.

These recipes aim to introduce readers to the delicious, healthful, longevity-boosting ingredients traditionally found in the Japanese diet, largely through applying them to familiar, Western dessert formats.

As Kyotofu's products have begun showing up on more and more grocery shelves across America, I have put together this cookbook as a means of giving curious home cooks access to the whole range of sweets we once served from our Manhattan restaurant. These recipes aim to introduce readers to the delicious, healthful, longevity-boosting ingredients traditionally found in the Japanese diet, largely through applying them to familiar, Western dessert formats. Kyotofu stands for dessert as part of a balanced, holistic approach to eating.

For those of us who grew up on brownies, cheesecake, cookies, and the like, Kyotofu's desserts combine something of the unique and the approachable. Take our Dark Chocolate Brownies (page 66), a graceful three-bite dessert made from dark chocolate and white miso, the traditional Japanese umami-booster.

紹介 INTRODUCTION

頁 17

本
KYOTOFU

頁
18

In contrast to the average sugar-riddled brownie the size of a roofing tile, this little ring-box-sized dessert is elegant in its simplicity and richly satisfying—not to mention fortified with antioxidants from high-quality dark chocolate as well as protein and immune-boosting properties courtesy of the miso.

I've lost almost eighty pounds since I began eating Japanese desserts as a regular part of my diet seven years ago.

Many of the ingredients used in this book carry proven nutritional benefits, ranging from fighting disease to bolstering brain function, which I touch upon throughout the text. Kyotofu's desserts also tend to be lower in sugar than typical Western recipes, and some are made using protein-rich tofu in the place of cream, butter, or eggs. I'm living proof of the transformational power of eating desserts the Japanese way: I've lost almost eighty pounds since I began eating Japanese desserts as a regular part of my diet seven years ago.

And lastly: While most dessert cookbooks are organized by format—a chapter for cookies, one for cakes, puddings, tarts, what have you—I've chosen to organize this one by ingredient. That's because I think it's the ingredients that make these desserts truly unique, whether it be the elegant citrus tang of yuzu or the nutty, earthy flavor of soy. Within each chapter, you'll find a range of different sweet ways to showcase my favorite Japanese food products. I hope you end up treasuring them as much as I do.

STOCKING A JAPANESE PANTRY

Although the majority of the ingredients used in this book are standard baking aisle provisions—flour, sugar, baking soda, chocolate—there are also a fair number of Japanese items that you may not have worked with before, and which you're unlikely to find at the average grocery store here in the United States. All of these items are listed and described below. While they may not be standard American supermarket fare, any of these ingredients are easily ordered online or purchased at a Japanese grocery store.

AGAR-AGAR: Also known as *kanten*, this clear, gelatinous substance is commonly used as a thickener in Japanese desserts and is a vegan alternative to gelatin. Agar-agar is obtained from algae, and it's sold in strips or as a powder. The recipes in this book all call for the powdered version.

AZUKI BEAN PASTE: Also called *anko*, azuki bean paste is made from boiling, mashing, and sweetening azuki red beans. It's a traditional and very prevalent ingredient in Japanese confectionary. There are several different varieties; *tsubu-an* is a chunky, coarse bean paste traditionally used as a dessert filling, whereas *koshi-an* is a smooth paste.

HOJICHA: This particular variety of green tea is made by roasting tea leaves over a charcoal fire, a process that turns the tea brown and burns off most of its caffeine, which results in a mild, mellow flavor. Ito En is my preferred brand.

IRI GENMAI: These toasted brown rice grains are typically sold in small pouches in a Japanese grocery's tea section. *Iri genmai* is traditionally mixed with green tea leaves to make a toasty, nutty tea called *genmaicha*. At Kyotofu, we use *iri genmai* in desserts to add texture and a pleasant roasted flavor to some of our baked goods.

JASMINE TEA: Green tea scented with Jasmine flower blossoms is Chinese in origin, but it's widely consumed in Okinawa, Japan. It's a gorgeous tea for drinking and figures into one recipe in this book (Jasmine Milk Chocolate Sweet Tofu, page 34). As with all teas, my preferred brand is Ito En.

KINAKO: Toasted soybeans are finely ground to make kinako, a flour with a nutty flavor similar to peanut butter. It's typically sold in small plastic packages and, due to its high oil content, should be stored in the refrigerator in an airtight container once opened.

KUROSATO: Japanese black sugar is unrefined cane sugar with a distinct dark molasses, malty flavor, and it's a very common ingredient in traditional Japanese desserts. *Kurosato* comes in little squares about the size and shape of Scrabble tiles, which are typically dissolved into liquid to form a syrup.

MATCHA: Earthy, bitter, antioxidant-packed matcha powder is milled from shade-grown green tea leaves (for more information on matcha, see page 80). I like Ito En brand best.

MISO: There are many different styles of miso (see page 54 for more information), but the only varieties we use at Kyotofu are conventional *shiro miso* (white miso) and a specialty type of *shiro miso* called *saikyo miso*. Both are very mild, gentle styles of miso. There are many good brands, but my favorite is Yamajirushi. Resealed properly after opening, miso can be stored in the refrigerator for months.

MOCHIKO: This sweet rice flour is made from ground, cooked glutinous (aka "sticky") rice and is traditionally mixed with water and sugar to make mochi. The resulting dough tends to be less sticky and easier to work with than dough made from *shiratamako* rice flour, but wrappers or candies made with mochiko have a shorter shelf life, as the dough usually hardens a day or two after they're made.

NASHI PEARS: Also called Asian pears in the United States, big, round Nashi pears combine the crisp texture of an apple with the flavor of a pear. These sweet, crunchy fruits are typically eaten fresh, but can be baked into pies or crumbles, too. Look for firm, heavy specimens without bruises or soft spots.

(Iri genmai)   (kinako)   (black sesame)

(jasmine tea)   (hoji-cha)   (matcha)

(Kura sato)   (shiratamako)   (Azuki)

PERSIMMONS: A favorite autumn flavor in Japan, persimmons look like orange-hued tomatoes and have a tart, almost apricot-like flavor. Persimmons must be eaten soft and ripe. The round Fuyu variety can be diced and eaten once they become tender; heart-shaped Hachiya persimmons are extremely astringent straight off the tree, and can't be eaten until their skin is wrinkled and their flesh spoonably soft.

SAKE: Sake is often referred to as "rice wine," although the brewing process is more similar to making beer. There are many different styles of sake, but the one I prefer to use in dessert recipes is *nigori* sake, or cloudy sake. I like it for its full body.

SESAME SEED PASTE: Made from finely-milled, toasted white or black sesame seeds, pungent sesame paste is the best way to incorporate a sesame flavor into ice creams, puddings, and mousses—anything where whole or ground seeds would interfere with the smooth texture of the finished product. Black and white pastes are typically packaged in small, spouted plastic pouches and should be refrigerated after opening.

SESAME SEEDS: Toasted black and white sesame seeds are commonly used in both sweet and savory dishes in Japan (for more information on sesame seeds, see page 96). You're unlikely to find black seeds outside of a Japanese grocery store; if you buy white sesame seeds elsewhere, they're likely to be untoasted, so remember to toast them in the oven or on the stovetop before use.

SHIRATAMAKO: This type of rice flour is made from uncooked, glutinous (aka "sticky") rice that has been washed, soaked in water, ground, and then pressed, dried, and crushed into course granules. *Shiratamako* differs from mochiko in that it creates a more elastic dough which, when molded into a mochi wrapper or candy, will stay soft and chewy for longer.

SILKEN TOFU: Tofu comes in different degrees of firmness. Silken tofu, which we use in some of our ice cream and cheesecake recipes, is the consistency of firm custard. I prefer House or Morinu brands.

SOY MILK: We use it to make our so-called sweet tofu panna cottas and to replace some, or all, of the dairy in ice creams, puddings, and sauces. Always buy an unsweetened variety. My favorite brand is Vitasoy; products imported from Japan have the highest soy content and tend to be the best. It's important to note that all commercially available soy milk is pasteurized, meaning that it can't be used to make tofu. For that, you need to make your own at home (or if you live near a sizeable Chinatown, look for fresh soy milk being sold there). A recipe for homemade soy milk can be found on page 39.

SUSHI RICE: Also called ordinary rice or *uruchimai* in Japan, this short-grained rice variety is the foundation of the Japanese diet. Sushi rice is distinct from so-called glutinous rice, which is produced in much smaller quantities in Japan and is used to make mochi. There are many different subvarieties of sushi rice, but for the purposes of this book, any will do. At a Japanese grocery store, sushi rice will simply be sold as white rice; at a general purpose supermarket, look for products marked sushi rice.

YUZU JUICE: The Japanese citrus fruit yuzu isn't readily available in the United States, but its tart juice can be found packaged in small glass bottles (for more information on yuzu, see page 134). Be sure to buy 100 percent pure yuzu juice, not juices mixed with salt or vinegar.

SOURCES

These days, most U.S. cities have at least one good Japanese grocery store where you can find all of the ingredients used in this book. A big city will have many to choose from. If you aren't able to locate a Japanese grocer, here are a few other resources that I've found handy for collecting ingredients.

Whole Foods: Whole Foods stores tend to carry a variety of Japanese ingredients (the exact assortment differs by store and region). I've had good luck finding miso, tofu, soy milk, sushi rice, persimmons, Nashi pears, and a wide selection of teas.

Mitsuwa: This small California-based chain of Japanese grocery stores has a wonderful website where you can buy shelf-stable pantry items online, from anywhere in the United States; www.mitsuwa.com.

Marukai: Another favorite Japanese supermarket chain, with stores in California and a good e-commerce site; www.marukaiestore.com.

Asian Food Grocer: One more valuable U.S.-based online resource for all sorts of Asian ingredients; www.asianfoodgrocer.com.

a note on

GLUTEN-FREE & VEGAN DESSERTS

Although gluten free is a foreign concept in Japan, the diet there is naturally very low in gluten, and I've made an effort for Kyotofu's desserts to reflect that reality. I've received tons of support in return from gluten-avoiding customers looking for high-quality, satisfying sweets that manage to avoid wheat, barley, and rye flours.

Almost all of the sweets in this book are either naturally gluten free or can be made gluten free by substituting my own flour mix—the recipe is printed on the following page—for all-purpose flour (look for the *gf* symbol throughout the book). Kyotofu's gluten-free flour is a cup-for-cup substitute, meaning that you simply swap an equal volume of this mix for conventional, all-purpose flour. How easy is that?

If you're buying premade gluten-free flour instead, I recommend Bob's Red Mill Gluten Free All-Purpose Baking Flour (also a cup-for-cup flour substitute). Whether you're using my mix or Bob's, keep in mind that a gluten-free mix isn't designed as a substitute for cake flour or bread flour—just all-purpose flour.

kyotofu gluten-free flour

We tried every gluten-free flour on the market before coming up with our own proprietary version, which we humbly believe to be better than anything else out there. Now we use this homemade blend in all our gluten-free treats. It's a cup-for-cup substitute for all-purpose flour, so you can easily substitute it in any recipe where all-purpose flour is listed (in this book, and beyond).

MAKES 6½ CUPS or 1 kg

2½ cups / 395 g brown rice flour

2½ cups / 395 g white rice flour

½ cup / 64 g cornstarch

½ cup / 63 g tapioca starch

½ cup / 90 g potato flour

2 tablespoons xanthan gum (optional)

1. Whisk together all of the ingredients until evenly combined and store in an airtight container in a cool, dark place for up to 2 months.

大豆

SOY

32	SWEET TOFU PUDDING WITH KUROMITSU SYRUP
34	JASMINE MILK CHOCOLATE SWEET TOFU
35	SOY MILK ICE CREAM WITH CHOCOLATE-KINAKO SYRUP
37	CHOCOLATE CHUNK COOKIES
38	SOY GINGERBREAD MEN
41	MAPLE PARFAIT
42	KINAKO WAFFLES WITH CHINESE FIVE-SPICE CREAM
45	CHOCOLATE TOFU ICE CREAM WITH UME CARAMEL SAUCE
47	DORAYAKI PANCAKES
48	JAPANESE MONT BLANCS
51	TOASTED SOY ICE CREAM

What's the first thing that comes to mind when you hear Japanese food? You probably think of sushi. Most people do. But I would argue that soybeans are even more central and essential to Japanese cuisine.

Soy is everywhere in Japan. Tofu is unpasteurized soy milk doctored with *nigari*, a special type of saltwater. Edamame are young soybeans. Miso is made from fermented soybeans, and so is soy sauce. Kinako is a special flour created by toasting soybeans and milling them until they're ground into a fine flour. Soybean pulp, or *okara*—the by-product of making soy milk—is a protein- and fiber-rich food that can be incorporated into fritters and baked goods like cupcakes and cookies. *Yuba* is the skin from the top of soy milk. The only soy product that doesn't have much of a place in the Japanese diet is soy milk. A nation of tea drinkers, the Japanese aren't really accustomed to the idea of drinking milk. Soy milk is primarily used to make tofu, and lately it's being churned into ice creams as well.

It's probably no coincidence, given the Japanese peoples' amazing track record for longevity, that soy is really healthy stuff. It's high in protein and also full of isoflavones, estrogen-like substances linked to the prevention of cancer and osteoporosis. Studies have shown that soy is heart healthy, too.

SOY

As a baker, I've found that soy is as beneficial for what it does contain as what it doesn't: Tofu and soy milk work wonders as creamy, silky, high-protein, low-fat and low cholesterol substitutes for eggs and dairy in desserts.

Whenever possible, buy soy-based ingredients that have been imported from Japan. Japanese soybeans are distinct from the ones grown in the Western hemisphere. Japan has never allowed genetically modified varieties into the country, and they prize flavor and nutrition in their soybeans over crop yields. As a result, quality is higher across the board. You can tell the difference just by looking at them: Japanese soybeans are perfectly round and unblemished, whereas beans grown in the United States tend to be knobbly and pockmarked.

When it comes to soy milk, Japan has regulations governing the minimum percentage of soybeans found in the milk, while U.S. manufacturers do not. This means that American versions can be very thin and lack the complex, nutty flavor of authentic Japanese soy milk.

sweet tofu pudding *with* kuromitsu syrup

While savory tofu has been a big part of the Japanese diet for centuries, so-called sweet tofu—which is really just soy milk, sweetened and then set with gelatin—is a relatively recent addition to the Japanese culinary landscape. A sort of Japanese version of a panna cotta, it's luscious, velvety, thick, yet remarkably light and protein rich. I like to serve it topped with a thin layer of kuromitsu, the molasses-like syrup that's very traditional in Japanese sweets. The effect reminds me of custardy crème caramel bathed in burnt caramel syrup.

MAKES 6

1 envelope powdered gelatin

2 cups / 475 ml soy milk

1/3 cup / 66 g granulated sugar

1/3 / 80 ml cup whole milk

1/2 cup / 120 ml heavy whipping cream

Kuromitsu Syrup to drizzle (page 169)

1. In a small bowl, sprinkle the gelatin over 1/4 cup / 60 ml of cold water and let stand for 5 minutes to soften.

2. Meanwhile, in a small saucepan combine 1 cup / 475 ml of the soy milk with the sugar over medium-low heat, and stir constantly, keeping the liquid below a simmer. Once all of the sugar has dissolved, remove the soy milk mixture from the heat.

3. Strain the gelatin through a fine mesh sieve to remove any standing water and add it to the hot soy milk, whisking well to dissolve fully. Add in the remaining soy milk, milk, and heavy whipping cream, stirring to incorporate. Divide the soy milk mixture between six individual ramekins, or small cups, and cover with plastic wrap.

4. Chill the ramekins in the refrigerator for at least 5 hours and up to 4 days.

5. Before serving, place the ramekins briefly in a warm water bath to unmold, and then invert the sweet tofu onto individual plates or a small bowl. Drizzle with the Kuromitsu Syrup and serve.

FOR A BLACK SESAME VARIATION: Use an additional 1/2 envelope of gelatin. Once all of the ingredients have been combined, cool the sweet tofu base in an ice bath until it thickens slightly, about 45 minutes. Add 1 tablespoon of black sesame paste and blend thoroughly with an immersion blender (or in the jar of a standard blender). Divide the sweet tofu base among the ramekins, cover them with plastic wrap, and continue to step 4.

章 SOY

頁 33

jasmine milk chocolate sweet tofu

This riff on our standard Sweet Tofu Pudding (page 32) pairs chocolate with Jasmine tea. Both are incredibly popular flavors in Japan, and I can't get over how perfectly the buttery taste of milk chocolate plays against Jasmine tea's floral, bitter notes.

SERVES 6

- 1 envelope powdered gelatin
- 2 cups / 475 ml soy milk
- 1/3 cup / 80 ml whole milk
- 1/4 cup / 50 g granulated sugar
- 1/3 cup / 45 g jasmine tea pearls
- 4 1/2 ounces / 128 g milk chocolate, chopped
- 2/3 cup / 160 ml heavy whipping cream

1. In a small bowl, sprinkle the gelatin over 1/4 cup 60 ml of cold water and let stand for 5 minutes to soften.

2. Meanwhile, combine the soy milk, whole milk, sugar, and tea in a small saucepan over medium-low heat, and bring the liquid to a simmer, stirring constantly. Remove the pan from the heat, cover, and steep the tea mixture for 15 minutes. Strain with a fine mesh sieve, reserving the liquid.

3. Break up the milk chocolate and place it in a heat-resistant bowl. In a small saucepan over medium heat, bring the heavy whipping cream to a boil. Pour the cream over the chocolate and let sit for 30 seconds. Stir the chocolate and cream together until well combined and the chocolate is fully melted.

4. Strain the gelatin through a fine mesh sieve to remove any standing water and add it to the hot soy milk, whisking well to dissolve fully. Slowly add the chocolate mixture, and stir to combine.

5. Divide the chocolate base between six ramekins, or small cups, and cover with plastic wrap. Chill in the refrigerator for at least 5 hours and up to 4 days.

6. Before serving, place the ramekins briefly in a warm water bath to unmold, and then invert the sweet tofu onto individual plates or a small bowl.

soy milk ice cream
with chocolate-kinako syrup

The taste of soy milk ice cream always brings me back to Kyoto, where little concessions stands and trinket shops line the pathways leading to the city's many shrines and temples. The sweet shops there will often have a soft-serve machine dispensing soy milk ice cream, which isn't really a cream at all: It's made from soy milk, whole milk, sugar, and eggs, just four ingredients that create something like a much lighter, cleaner version of vanilla ice cream. I find that it satisfies my sweet tooth without leaving me overfull.

MAKES 1 PINT or 475 ml

- ⅔ cup / 160 ml soy milk
- 1¼ cups / 295 ml whole milk
- ½ cup / 99 g granulated sugar
- Pinch salt
- 5 large egg yolks
- Chocolate-Kinako Syrup (page 160)

1. Fill a large bowl with ice and cold water and set aside.

2. In a medium saucepan, combine the soy milk, whole milk, sugar, and salt over medium heat, and bring to a simmer, for about 5 minutes.

3. In a separate bowl, whisk the egg yolks together. Whisking constantly, gradually pour half of the hot milk mixture into the yolks. Return the yolk mixture to the saucepan and cook over low heat, stirring constantly with a wooden spoon or heat-resistant spatula, or until the custard thickens enough to coat the back of a spoon, 3 to 5 minutes.

4. Transfer the custard to a heat-resistant container in the ice bath, and stir frequently until it cools to room temperature. Cover with plastic wrap and chill thoroughly in the refrigerator.

5. Freeze in an ice cream machine according to the manufacturer's instructions. Serve topped with Chocolate-Kinako Syrup.

Due to its low-fat content, this ice cream is best enjoyed straight from the machine. The soft creaminess won't last stored in your freezer.

本 KYOTOFU

chocolate chunk cookies

As far as I'm concerned, no dessert book would be complete without a chocolate chip cookie recipe. The quintessentially American treat takes on a Japanese twist with the addition of kinako —roasted soybean flour—which has a peanutty flavor that pairs amazingly well with dark chocolate.

MAKES ABOUT 20 COOKIES

- 1½ cups / 180 g all-purpose flour
- ⅓ cup / 47 g kinako
- ½ teaspoon baking soda
- 1 teaspoons salt
- ½ cup (1 stick) / 113 g unsalted butter, softened
- ⅓ cup / 66 g granulated sugar
- ½ cup / 109 g light brown sugar
- 1 large egg
- ½ teaspoon vanilla extract
- 4½ ounces / 128 g dark chocolate (64% cacao), roughly chopped

1. Preheat the oven to 350° F / 177°C. In a medium bowl, whisk together the flour, kinako, baking soda, and salt, and set aside.

2. In the bowl of an electric mixer fitted with a paddle attachment, cream together the butter and sugars on medium-high speed until pale and fluffy, 5 to 7 minutes. Add in the egg and the vanilla extract and mix well.

3. Add the dry ingredients in several additions, mixing just until incorporated. Fold the chocolate chunks into the dough; wrap the dough in plastic wrap and chill in the refrigerator for at least 30 minutes and up to 2 days.

4. Drop the chilled dough by rounded tablespoons onto baking sheets and bake for 12 to 15 minutes, or until golden-brown.

soy gingerbread men gf

These cookies are a seasonal bestseller for Kyotofu. Adding in kinako, the nutty roasted soybean flour, delivers a simple little spin on the gingerbread man cookies that everyone knows and loves at Christmastime.

MAKES ABOUT 24 COOKIES

¼ cup / 36 g kinako

4 cups / 480 g all-purpose flour

½ teaspoon baking soda

¼ teaspoon baking powder

½ cup (1 stick) / 113 g unsalted butter, softened

½ cup / 109 g light brown sugar

2 teaspoons ground ginger

1 teaspoon ground cinnamon

¾ teaspoon ground cloves

½ teaspoon ground black pepper

¾ teaspoon salt

1 large egg

½ cup / 120 ml blackstrap molasses

Red sanding sugar, for sprinkling

1. Preheat the oven to 350° F / 177°C. In a large bowl, sift together the kinako, all-purpose flour, baking soda, and baking powder and set aside.

2. In the bowl of an electric mixer fitted with a paddle attachment, cream together the butter and brown sugar until fluffy, about 5 minutes. Add the ginger, cinnamon, cloves, black pepper, and salt, and mix until fully incorporated. Add the egg and the molasses, mixing well after each addition.

3. With the mixer speed on low, add the dry ingredients, mixing until just combined.

4. Divide the dough into four disks, wrap each disk in plastic wrap, and chill in the refrigerator for at least 30 minutes.

5. On a floured work surface, working with one disk of dough at a time, roll out the dough to a ¼-inch / .5 cm thickness. Stamp out the cookies using a floured 3-inch / 7.5 cm gingerbread man cutter and place them on a baking sheet. Sprinkle the cookies with red sanding sugar. Bake for 5 to 6 minutes (longer if you're using a larger gingerbread man cutter), or until slightly brown around the edges.

MAKING SOY MILK AT HOME

Making your own soy milk is fast, easy, and cheap, and you might be surprised to discover how much tastier the finished product is than what you buy in the store. I find that commercial varieties sold in America tend to be watery compared to the soy milk you get in Japan. Fresh soy milk is wonderful to drink on its own or to use for the recipes in this book.

Since soy milk consists of only two things—soybeans and water—it's important that each of those ingredients is of the highest quality possible. Be sure to start with Japanese soybeans (ideally, organic ones), which you can buy at any Asian grocery store. Try to use only filtered water, as any off flavor in the water will really come across in the finished soy milk. The recipe below makes about a quart of soy milk, which can be stored in the refrigerator for up to 4 days.

½ cup/88g dried soybeans

1. Soak ½ cup / 88 g dried soybeans in filtered water for 8 hours; the beans will double or triple in size. Drain and rinse the beans.

2. Transfer the beans to a blender, adding 3½ cups / 830 ml filtered water for every cup of soaked beans. Puree the mixture for 3 to 4 minutes, or until very smooth. Place a mesh sieve and several thicknesses of cheesecloth over a medium-sized pot, gathering up the cheesecloth and squeezing gently to force the liquid through.

3. Bring the strained soy milk to a simmer over medium heat. Let simmer for 20 minutes, skimming off the skin that accumulates on the surface from time to time.

4. Pass the finished soy milk through a mesh sieve one last time, let cool, and refrigerate.

本

K
Y
O
T
O
F
U

maple parfait

This creamy parfait is designed to be frozen in molds rather than spun in an ice cream maker, making it a delicious summer dessert option for home cooks who don't have access to an ice cream machine. Its texture is best if it's given time to thaw slightly before serving, rather than being served straight from the freezer.

SERVES 8 to 10

- ⅔ cup / 76 g cashews
- 3 large egg yolks
- ½ cup / 99 g sugar
- 1 cup / 235 ml Soy Curd (page 171)
- ¼ cup / 60 ml maple syrup
- 2 teaspoons vanilla extract
- 1⅔ cups / 395 ml heavy whipping cream
- Passion Fruit Crème Anglaise (page 159)

1. Preheat the oven to 350° F / 177°C. Toast the cashews on a baking sheet for about 5 minutes, or until they become fragrant and brown. Remove the cashews from the oven and let cool slightly. Chop coarsely and set aside.

2. In the bowl of an electric mixer fitted with a paddle attachment, whip the egg yolks until pale and ribbony.

3. Meanwhile, mix the sugar with ¼ cup / 60 ml water in a small saucepan fitted with a candy thermometer over medium-high heat and bring to a boil, swirling the pan to help the sugar dissolve. When the candy thermometer reaches 240° F / 116°C or the syrup can be formed into a soft ball in cold water, remove the hot sugar from the heat and carefully pour it into the egg yolks in a bowl of an electric mixer on high speed.

4. Reduce the mixer speed to low and add the Soy Curd, maple syrup, and vanilla extract, mixing well. Fold in the cashews.

5. In a separate bowl, whip the heavy whipping cream until it forms stiff peaks, and then fold it into the batter.

6. Spoon the batter into muffin tins, filling each tin to the top and squaring it off with a knife or bench scraper. Freeze the parfaits for at least 6 hours, preferably overnight.

7. Before serving, let the parfaits stand at room temperature for around 10 minutes to soften. Spoon a pool of Passion Fruit Crème Anglaise onto each dessert plate. Running a warm knife around the edge of each parfait to help release it from the pan, place a parfait on top of the anglaise.

kinako waffles
with chinese five-spice cream

Waffles are popular in Japan, but they're always eaten as a snack or dessert—never for breakfast, which tends to be dominated by savory foods rather than sweets. This version is a little different from standard American recipes in that it uses kinako flour to give the batter a deliciously nutty, rich, toasted dimension.

SERVES 8

1½ cups / 180 g all-purpose flour

½ cup / 71 g kinako, plus 2 tablespoons for dusting

1 tablespoon granulated sugar

4 teaspoons baking powder

1 teaspoon cinnamon

¼ teaspoon salt

2 large eggs

½ cup / 120 ml soy milk

1 cup / 235 ml whole milk

½ can (7 ounces / 198 g) sweetened condensed milk

½ teaspoon vanilla extract

2 tablespoons confectioners' sugar

Chinese Five-Spice Cream (recipe follows)

Maple syrup, to taste

1. In a large bowl, mix together the all-purpose flour, ½ cup / 71 g kinako, granulated sugar, baking powder, cinnamon, and salt. Add the eggs, soy milk, whole milk, condensed milk, and vanilla extract, and mix until well combined.

2. Spoon the batter into a waffle maker and cook according to the manufacturer's instructions.

3. Whisk together 2 tablespoons kinako with 2 tablespoons confectioner's sugar, and, using a fine mesh sieve, dust the sugar mixture over the finished waffles. Add a dollop of Chinese Five-Spice Cream and drizzle with maple syrup. Serve immediately.

SOY

chinese five-spice cream

MAKES 2 CUPS or 475 ml

1 cup / 235 ml heavy whipping cream

2 teaspoons confectioners' sugar

1 teaspoon Chinese five-spice powder

1. Pour the heavy whipping cream into a large bowl and whisk in the confectioners' sugar and Chinese five-spice powder. Whip by hand or with a handheld electric mixer until stiff peaks form. Use immediately.

chocolate tofu ice cream
with ume caramel sauce

We developed this recipe because customers were clamoring for a dairy- and gluten-free frozen treat (if you substitute agave nectar for the honey, the recipe becomes fully vegan). While this faux ice cream isn't something with direct roots in Japan, it does showcase the incredible versatility of tofu: Here, it makes a pretty darn convincing stand-in for the heavy whipping cream and egg yolks that give regular ice cream its body. Low in fat and sugar and high in protein and antioxidants, you can't find a healthier option for dessert.

MAKES 1 PINT or 475 ml

¼ medium ripe banana, sliced

2½ tablespoons honey (agave nectar may be substituted)

1 tablespoon cocoa powder

2 tablespoons kinako

1½ cups / 348 g silken tofu

1½ ounces / 43 g dark chocolate, chopped (64% cacao)

Ume Caramel Sauce (page 164)

1. In the bowl of a food processor, combine the banana, honey, cocoa powder, kinako, and tofu and blend until creamy and smooth.

2. In a glass bowl, microwave the chocolate in 30 seconds increments until fully melted; stir the chocolate with a rubber spatula between heatings. Add the melted chocolate to the tofu mixture and process until fully incorporated.

3. Freeze in an ice cream machine according to the manufacturer's instructions. Serve topped with Ume Caramel Sauce.

Due to its low-fat content, this ice cream is best enjoyed straight from the machine. Once stored in your freezer, its initial soft creaminess won't last.

本
KYOTOFU

dorayaki pancakes gf

Dorayaki are a type of wagashi, or tea sweet, made by sandwiching red bean paste between two bite-sized pancakes made from a special type of sponge cake. This miniature confection was the inspiration behind these extra-fluffy breakfast pancakes that feature Japanese ingredients like honey and mirin rice wine but are designed to be eaten in the usual American way.

SERVES 4

2 large eggs, whites and yolks separated

1 cup / 120 g all-purpose flour

½ teaspoon baking powder

½ teaspoon salt

½ cup / 99 g granulated sugar

2 tablespoons soy milk

1 ½ tablespoons unsalted butter, melted

2 teaspoons mirin

2 teaspoons honey

Maple syrup, to taste

1. In a medium bowl, whip the egg whites until stiff peaks form. In a small bowl, whisk the yolks together. Set both bowls aside.

2. In a large bowl, sift together the flour, baking powder, salt, and sugar. Make a well in the center of the dry ingredients and pour in the soy milk, egg yolks, melted butter, mirin, and honey, and mix until smooth. Fold in the egg whites.

3. Heat a lightly-oiled griddle or nonstick frying pan over medium-high heat. Pour or scoop the batter onto the griddle, using approximately ¼ cup / 60 ml of batter for each pancake. Flip the pancakes once they have browned on the bottom, after about 3 minutes. Cook for 3 to 4 minutes more, or until both sides are golden-brown and the batter is cooked through. Place the pancakes on plates and serve drizzled with maple syrup.

japanese mont blancs

In the basements of Tokyo's department stores, you'll find food courts called **depachikas** *filled with football fields worth of raw and prepared foods, from spices and teas to pickled vegetables, dumplings, and sushi. Sweet confections are arranged in display cases worthy of a jewelry store; amid the tarts, mousses, and macarons you will always find mont blancs, the European chestnut cream cakes named after the snow-capped mountain that straddles the French and Italian border. This is a recipe for the classic version, although in Japan you also sometimes see matcha added in, or sweet potato, pumpkin, or strawberry used in the place of chestnut.*

SERVES 12

- ½ cup / 60 g all-purpose flour
- 1 cup / 142 g plus 2 tablespoons kinako
- 2 teaspoons baking powder
- 1 teaspoon salt
- ½ cup (1 stick) / 113 g unsalted butter, softened
- 2 large eggs
- ⅓ cup / 80 ml maple syrup
- ⅓ cup / 80 ml soy milk
- 8 chestnuts in syrup, chopped
- Chestnut Mousse (recipe follows)
- 8 whole chestnuts in syrup

1. Preheat the oven to 350° F / 177°C. Grease, with nonstick spray or butter, and flour a muffin tin. In a medium bowl, whisk together the all-purpose flour, kinako, baking powder, and salt.

2. In the bowl of an electric mixer fitted with a paddle attachment, whip the butter until light and fluffy, 5 minutes. Beat in the eggs, one at a time, and then stir in the maple syrup. Add in the flour mixture and mix until just combined. Stir in the soy milk by hand until the batter is smooth. Fold in the chopped chestnuts. Pour or spoon the batter into 12 prepared muffin molds.

3. Bake for 16 to 18 minutes, or until the cakes spring back to the touch. Remove the cakes from the oven and let them cool to room temperature.

4. Using a pastry bag fitted with a small basketweave pastry tip, pipe the Chestnut Mousse onto the cakes in ribbons, creating a domed peak. Top each with a chestnut and serve.

49

chestnut mousse

MAKES 3 CUPS or 710 ml

- 1 tablespoon powdered gelatin
- 1/3 cup / 80 ml heavy whipping cream
- 1/4 cup / 50 g granulated sugar
- 1/3 cup / 80 g vanilla-flavored candied chestnut paste
- 1 tablespoon sake
- 3 large egg whites, whipped to stiff peaks

1. In a small bowl, sprinkle the gelatin over 1/4 cup / 60 ml of cold water and let it stand for 5 minutes to soften.

2. Meanwhile, bring the heavy whipping cream and sugar to a boil in a small saucepan over medium-high heat, about 5 minutes. In a separate bowl, whisk together the chestnut paste and sake. Whisk the bloomed gelatin into the chestnut paste, and then pour the hot cream in gradually. Let the mixture cool slightly.

3. Fold the whipped egg whites into the chestnut mixture, cover with plastic wrap, and let chill in the refrigerator until firm, at least 1 hour.

toasted soy ice cream

This frozen treat has many of the same health advantages of Chocolate Tofu Ice Cream (page 45) without going totally dairy free. If you're okay with including a small amount of heavy whipping cream, it gives the ice cream a richer, rounder, more buttery flavor than can be achieved with tofu alone.

MAKES 1 PINT or 475 ml

- 3 tablespoons honey
- 4 tablespoons brown sugar
- ½ cup / 120 ml heavy whipping cream
- 1⅓ cups / 309 g silken tofu
- 3 tablespoons kinako

1. Combine the honey, brown sugar, and heavy whipping cream in a medium saucepan over medium heat. Heat the mixture until the sugar and honey have melted into the cream.

2. Transfer the cream mixture to the bowl of a blender or food processor and add the tofu and kinako, blending the ingredients until smooth.

3. Freeze the mixture in an ice cream machine according to the manufacturer's instructions.

Due to its low-fat content, this ice cream is best enjoyed straight from the machine. Stored in your freezer, the initial soft creaminess won't last.

味噌

MISO

| 56 | CHOCOLATE SOUFFLÉ CUPCAKES WITH SHIRO-AN CREAM
| 58 | SWEET MISO ICE CREAM WITH SAFFRON CARAMEL SAUCE
| 61 | RASPBERRY CHEESECAKE
| 62 | WARM PERSIMMON MOCHI CHOCOLATE CAKE
| 64 | CHOCOLATE TART
| 66 | DARK CHOCOLATE BROWNIES

Miso is my "magic" ingredient: a seasoning that deepens and expands the flavor of almost anything it touches.

Made from a mix of grains (barley, rice, buckwheat, rye, and wheat are common), cooked soybeans, and sea salt, miso is packed into wooden barrels along with a starter fungus and left to ferment for anywhere from a few months to a few years (it's tastier than it sounds—I promise!). The result is a richly-flavored paste that can vary from a salty, buttery character to one that's deeply beefy and pungent. There are lots of factors that impact what the final product will taste like, from the exact mix of grains to what starter culture is used, what sort of water is added, and maybe most critically, how long the miso is aged.

Countless recipes yield all kinds of unique flavor profiles. The Japanese eat very regionally, and different parts of Japan have their own traditional miso preparations, all with their own distinct flavors. There are commercial misos available at supermarkets and convenience stores, as well as rarified artisanal versions that command high prices.

MISO IS BROADLY CLASSIFIED INTO A THREE TYPES:

Shiro miso (white miso)—The most subtle and mild type of miso.

Shinshu miso (yellow miso)—Fermented slightly longer than white miso, yellow misos are a little bit saltier and more savory.

Aka miso (red miso)—The most pungent of them all, red misos ferment for as long as three years and are typically paired with bolder flavors, like grilled meats.

Generally speaking, the darker in color the miso, the saltier and bolder it tastes.

In Japan, a traditional Japanese breakfast always includes miso soup, which is made by mixing miso paste into dashi stock. Miso is used in sauces, meat and fish marinades, and as a glaze for meats and o*nigiri* rice balls cooked on yakitori grills. The goal with miso is to always enhance and deepen the other flavors present.

Back in the United States, I couldn't wait to experiment with new, unusual ways to deploy miso. The brash, salty paste is never paired with sweet ingredients in Japan (credit the strength of convention here), but I always thought that it would go well with chocolate—salted chocolate is a popular combination after all, and miso adds a deliciously buttery dimension as well. It pairs beautifully with caramel and with vanilla, too, for the same reason. As an added benefit, miso is a natural preservative, so anything you add it to will stay fresh for longer.

Experimentation has taught me that white miso does the best in desserts; yellow and red varieties can be too funky. There's a specialty white miso called *saikyo miso* (sweet miso), which happens to originate in Kyoto and is a particular favorite of mine in desserts.

Like so many Japanese ingredients, miso is healthy as well as delicious. It's full of probiotics, which help maintain digestive health. It's high in protein, but also in sodium—which is why I use it sparingly, and in place of salt in a recipe. For me, miso is like bacon: a little bit goes a long way.

chocolate soufflé cupcakes *gf*
with shiro-an cream

Most chocolate cupcake recipes call for only cocoa powder, but I use high-quality melted chocolate in Kyotofu's version. I find that it imparts a much more potent and nuanced flavor than cocoa alone (and if you're going to eat chocolate, you might as well really go for it, right?). But the real secret to these cupcakes, which were once ranked the city's best by New York Magazine, is miso: the salty, buttery paste intensifies their chocolate flavor in a big way.

MAKES 12 CUPCAKES

7 ounces / 198 g dark chocolate, chopped (64% cacao)

7 ounces / 198 g (1 3/4 sticks) unsalted butter

1 1/2 tablespoons white miso paste

1 1/3 cup / 153 g confectioners' sugar

1/4 cup / 30 g all-purpose flour

1/4 cup / 31 g bread flour

2 tablespoons cocoa powder

3/4 teaspoon baking powder

1/4 teaspoon salt

4 large eggs, at room temperature

Shiro-An Cream (page 156)

1. Preheat the oven to 325° F / 163°C. Melt the chocolate, butter, and miso in a double boiler set over simmering water. Once melted and smooth, transfer the chocolate mixture to a large mixing bowl.

2. In a separate medium bowl, sift together the confectioners' sugar, flours, cocoa powder, baking powder, and salt. Add the melted chocolate in several additions, mixing constantly. Whisk in the eggs one at a time.

3. Prepare a cupcake tin by lining the molds with cupcake liners. Divide the batter between the cupcake molds and bake for 18 to 20 minutes, or until a cake tester comes out clean. Remove from the oven, let cool, and serve frosted with Shiro-An Cream.

章 MISO

頁 57

sweet miso ice cream
with saffron caramel sauce

Sweeter and less salty than standard shiro miso, saikyo miso is a product native to Kyoto (a city that, due to its amazing artisan food culture, has a special place in my heart). It lends this low-fat ice cream an incredibly round, rich, butterscotch flavor.

MAKES 1 3/4 CUPS or 415 ml

½ cup / 120 ml soy milk

1 cup / 235 ml whole milk

⅓ cup / 66 g sugar

4 large egg yolks

1 tablespoon saikyo miso

Saffron Caramel Sauce (page 162)

1. Fill a large bowl with ice and cold water and set aside.

2. Combine the soy milk, whole milk, and sugar in a medium saucepan over medium heat, and simmer about 5 minutes.

3. In a separate bowl, whisk together the egg yolks and miso. Whisking constantly, gradually pour about half the hot milk mixture into the yolk mixture. Stir the warmed yolks and milk back into the saucepan and cook them over low heat; stir constantly with a wooden spoon or heat-resistant spatula, or until the custard thickens enough to coat the back of a spoon, 3 to 5 minutes.

4. Transfer the custard to a heat-resistant container set in the ice bath; stir the custard frequently until it cools to room temperature. Cover with plastic wrap and chill thoroughly in the refrigerator.

5. Freeze the custard in an ice cream machine according to the manufacturer's instructions, and serve topped with Saffron Caramel Sauce.

Due to the low-fat content of the ice cream, it is best enjoyed straight from the ice cream machine. Stored in your freezer, its initial soft, creaminess will turn hard.

FEEDING BEAUTIFUL SKIN

Japanese women are famous the world over for their astonishingly youthful, flawless skin, and it's no mystery how they manage to maintain to the complexion of a 25-year-old well into middle age. Not only do they tend to approach personal grooming with an unrivaled level of care and devotion, but the Japanese feast every day on a pantry of singularly skin-enriching foods. Their diet plays a major role in preserving and nourishing those glowing complexions.

Miso, for instance, has been shown to reduce signs of skin aging. The fermented soybean paste slows the appearance of fine lines and wrinkles by increasing the skin's production of hyaluronic acid, which helps maintain firm, healthy skin.

Vitamin and antioxidant-rich seaweed, a Japanese dietary staple, has been shown to promote skin elasticity while reducing inflammation and redness. And all that green tea that the Japanese drink? It arms them with protection against wrinkle-inducing ultraviolet rays, and helps to rejuvenate aging skin cells. The Japanese diet is also rich in fish, whose Omega-3 fatty acids keep skin hydrated and glowing.

Beyond all of the beauty benefits conferred by eating foods like these, some Japanese edibles also play a topical role in skincare routines. In the middle of winter, for instance, it's traditional in Japan to take a hot bath filled with the citrus fruit yuzu. The oils from yuzu are thought to help soothe and soften chapped skin, as well as to promote good circulation.

Azuki beans, the red legumes mashed into a paste for use in many classic Japanese desserts, are also ground and used to make a special exfoliating face scrub. Wakame seaweed is traditionally used to make a detoxifying face gel. For generations, Japanese women have used rice bran oil as a moisturizer and makeup remover, and stone-ground rice bran powder as a cleanser and wrinkle-reducer. In fact, in Japan it's a high compliment to be called a *nuka bijin*: literally, a "rice bran beauty."

本
KYOTOFU

raspberry cheesecake

Cheese isn't a part of the traditional Japanese diet, and yet strangely enough, you see cheesecakes everywhere in today's Japan. The format is pure Americana, of course, but the Japanese version is lighter and airier than the dense, sweet preparations that we tend to gravitate to here in the States. People rave about this Japanese-inspired raspberry version and often ask me what that "extra something" is in its flavor. You guessed it: miso.

SERVES 16

- 2 cups / 200 g graham cracker crumbs, from about 16 crackers
- Pinch salt
- ½ cup (1 stick) / 113 g unsalted butter, melted and cooled slightly
- ¾ cup / 90 g raspberries
- 1 cup / 198 g plus 2 tablespoons granulated sugar, divided
- 3 cups (22 ounces / 624 g) cream cheese, at room temperature
- 1½ tablespoons shiro miso
- ½ teaspoon vanilla extract
- 3 large eggs, at room temperature

1. Preheat the oven to 350° F / 177°C. Wrap the bottom of a 9-inch / 23 cm springform pan in two layers of aluminum foil to prevent water from leaking in at the seams.

2. In the bowl of a food processor, process the graham crackers into fine, sandy crumbs. In a medium bowl, combine the graham cracker crumbs with the salt and melted butter, and then press the mixture into the bottom and about 1 inch / 2.5 cm up the sides of the springform pan. Bake the crust for 10 minutes, remove from the oven, and let cool to room temperature. Lower the oven temperature to 325° F / 163°C.

3. Puree the raspberries in a food processor or blender and pass them through a fine mesh sieve, discarding the seeds. Stir in 2 tablespoons of sugar and set the puree aside.

4. In the bowl of an electric mixer fitted with a paddle attachment, combine the sugar and cream cheese and mix on medium speed until light and fluffy, 3 to 5 minutes, scraping down the sides of the bowl halfway through. Add the miso, vanilla extract, eggs, and raspberry puree. Pour the batter into the prepared crust.

5. Place the springform pan inside a high-sided roasting pan and pour boiling water halfway up the side of the pan. Bake the cheesecake for 90 minutes, then turn off the heat and leave the oven door cracked slightly, allowing the cake to cool slowly to prevent cracking. Chill in the refrigerator for at least 4 hours before serving.

warm persimmon mochi chocolate cake

If you've ever come in contact with mochi—the gummy confection made from rice flour—it's probably been as a soft, chewy covering for ice cream. This dessert puts mochi on the inside rather than the outside, giving a petite chocolate cake a soft, fruity, surprise center.

Serves 10

7 ounces / 198 g dark chocolate, chopped (64% cacao)

7 ounces / 198 g (1¾ sticks) unsalted butter

2 tablespoons shiro miso

1½ cup / 173 g confectioners' sugar

5 tablespoons all-purpose flour

3 tablespoons cocoa powder

4 large eggs

Persimmon Mochi (recipe follows)

Kuro Crème Anglaise (page 165)

Matcha Shiro-An Cream (page 156)

1. Preheat the oven to 350° F / 177°C. In a double boiler set over medium heat, melt together the chocolate, butter, and miso, whisking the mixture until smooth.

2. In a medium bowl, whisk together the confectioners' sugar, flour, and cocoa powder. Gradually stir the dry ingredients into the melted chocolate mixture. Remove the batter from the heat and whisk in the eggs one at a time.

3. Place cupcake liners in 10 cupcake molds. Divide the batter between the 10 molds.

4. Dip your fingers in cornstarch and pinch off a bit of Persimmon Mochi slightly smaller than a marble. Roll it into a ball and gently insert it into one of the wells of batter. Repeat with all 10 cakes. Bake for 15 to 18 minutes, or until the cakes are slightly firm to the touch. Remove from the oven and let cool slightly.

5. Spoon a pool of Kuro Crème Anglaise onto a plate, then remove the cupcake liner from one of the cakes and place the cake on top. Top with Matcha Shiro-An Cream. Repeat with the remaining cakes, and serve immediately.

persimmon mochi

MAKES 1/3 CUP or 80 ml

¼ cup / 30 g shiratamako flour

2 tablespoons persimmon flesh (see note)

¼ cup / 50 g granulated sugar

Cornstarch to dust

1. In a small bowl, mix the *shiratamako* with 2 tablespoons water and knead with your hands until smooth and elastic. Add the persimmon puree and then the sugar, stirring until fully incorporated.

2. In a small nonstick skillet set over medium heat, heat the *shiratamako* mixture, stirring constantly with a wooden spoon or rubber spatula until firm, gooey, and translucent, 3 to 5 minutes. Scrape the mochi dough into a small bowl dusted with cornstarch and let cool in the refrigerator for at least half an hour before using.

Start with a very ripe Hachiya persimmon, cut it in half, and spoon out 2 tablespoons of flesh. For an extra-smooth finished product or if the persimmon flesh isn't spoonably soft, puree the flesh in a food processor, strain it through a fine mesh sieve, and measure out 2 tablespoons.

chocolate tart ⓖⓕ

For the serious chocolate addict, this tart is about as dense and decadent as it gets, laced with salty, buttery miso to achieve an unbelievable depth of flavor. It's also a thing of beauty, with a satiny surface worthy of pastry case display.

SERVES 8

½ cup / 55 g cake flour

¾ cup / 94 g bread flour

¼ cup / 30 g cocoa powder

½ cup / 58 g plus 1 tablespoon confectioners' sugar

½ teaspoon salt

½ cup (1 stick) / 113 g unsalted butter, chilled, cut into 12 pieces

2 large eggs yolks

¾ teaspoon vanilla extract

1 cup / 235 ml plus 2 tablespoons heavy whipping cream

⅓ cup / 80 ml whole milk

1½ tablespoons simple syrup

7 ounces / 198 g dark chocolate, chopped (64% cacao)

1 large egg

2 teaspoons shiro miso

1. For the tart crust: Place the flours, cocoa powder, confectioners' sugar, and salt in the bowl of a food processor and pulse to combine. Add the butter and pulse for about 10 seconds, or until the mixture resembles coarse meal. Add the egg yolks and vanilla extract and process until the mixture forms into a ball. Remove the ball from the food processor, flatten it into a disk, wrap tightly in plastic wrap, and let chill in the refrigerator for 30 minutes.

2. Preheat the oven to 350° F / 177°C. On a floured work surface, roll out the dough to ¼-inch / .5 cm thickness and/or press it directly into a greased 9-inch / 23 cm tart pan. Cover the crust with parchment paper filled with pie weights and bake for 30 minutes. Remove the crust from the oven and let cool to room temperature, lowering the oven temperature to 275° F / 135°C.

3. For the filling: Combine the cream, milk, and simple syrup in a medium saucepan over medium heat. Stirring occasionally, heat the liquid for 3 to 5 minutes, or until it's just below a simmer.

4. Break the chocolate into small pieces and place them in a medium-sized, heat-resistant bowl. In a separate bowl, whisk together the egg and the miso. Whisking constantly, gradually pour the hot milk mixture into the egg mixture.

5. Pour the cream mixture over the chocolate and let sit for one minute. Blend the mixture with an inversion blender until smooth, and then strain through a fine mesh sieve. Pour the filling into the crust.

6. Bake the tart for 25 to 30 minutes, or until filling is fully set and doesn't jiggle when you shake it. Let cool for at least 2 hours and serve cold or at room temperature.

章 MISO

頁

dark chocolate brownies ⏵

This recipe is similar to the one for Chocolate Soufflé Cupcakes (page 56), except for the baking powder, without which the batter stays dense and fudgy instead of puffing up into an airy cupcake. As for the cupcakes, miso sets these brownies apart from the pack; its salty, buttery, complex undertones really amp up their chocolate richness.

MAKES 16 BROWNIES

- 7 ounces / 198 g dark chocolate, chopped (64% cacao)
- 7 ounces / 198 g (1¾ sticks) unsalted butter
- 3 tablespoons plus 1 teaspoon white miso paste
- 1 cup / 115 g plus 2 tablespoons confectioners' sugar
- 5 tablespoons all-purpose flour
- 8 teaspoons cocoa powder
- 4 large eggs, at room temperature

1. Preheat the oven to 350° F / 177°C. Lightly grease an 8 x 8-inch / 20 x 20 cm baking pan. Melt the chocolate, butter, and miso in a double boiler over simmering water.

2. Meanwhile, whisk the confectioners' sugar, flour, and cocoa powder in a medium bowl. Gradually whisk the dry ingredients into the melted chocolate mixture.

3. Remove the batter from heat and whisk in the eggs one at a time. Transfer the batter to the prepared pan and bake for 35 to 40 minutes, or until a cake tester comes out clean.

FOR A PEPPERMINT VARIATION: Halve the quantity of miso and add 2 teaspoons of peppermint oil at the same time the eggs are added.

FOR A CHAI VARIATION: Halve the quantity of miso and add 1½ tablespoons chai tea powder, 1 teaspoon ground cardamom, 1 teaspoon ground cinnamon, ½ teaspoon cloves, and ½ teaspoon nutmeg along with the dry ingredients.

章 MISO

緑茶

GREEN TEA

72	MATCHA CRÈME BRÛLÉE
74	GREEN TEA CAKE WITH GINGER MOUSSE
76	JAPANESE TOAST
78	GREEN TEA CHOCOLATE CAKES
79	HOJICHA ICE CREAM
83	GREEN TEA WHITE CHOCOLATE CUPCAKES
84	MATCHA "RARE" CHEECAKE
86	MATCHA ICE CREAM
87	GREEN TEA MUFFINS
89	TOKYO TIRAMISU
90	GREEN TEA YOKAN
93	HOJI ROLL CAKE

Green tea is, bar none, the most commonly consumed beverage in Japan. Nothing else even comes close.

That fact can be difficult to wrap your head around coming from the United States, where we like to have such a vast variety of thirst-quenching options—whole grocery store aisles full of fruit juices, milks, coffee drinks, sodas, and sports drinks competing with quiet, unassuming tea for our attention. Well, the Japanese drink more green tea than all of those other categories combined.

Green tea is believed to have arrived in Japan from China in the twelfth century, where it was soon cultivated and incorporated into the Japanese diet. Visit a Japanese market today and you'll see a wide range of green tea varieties, distinct from each other in terms of how and where the tea plant is grown, which parts of it are used, and how it's processed.

A couple of the recipes in this chapter call for *hojicha*, a type of green tea with its roots in Kyoto (for more on *hojicha*, see page 81). But when we talk about green tea in this book, we're mostly talking about a very specific product called matcha: the highly potent, concentrated green tea powder.

While green tea is grown and consumed all across Asia, matcha is a product that's unique to Japan. Matcha is made from green tea leaves that have been grown in the shade, making them intensely green in color. The tea is harvested and the stems removed by hand before it is dried and slowly milled in a purpose-built grinder into a fine powder. There are several different grades of matcha, based on the quality of the leaves and what part of the country they're grown in. No matter what the grade, matcha is extremely expensive; it rarely sells for less than fifty dollars per pound, and often for much more.

Matcha's historical use was as a part of ritualistic tea ceremonies. The bitter, earthy powder was whisked into hot water (matcha doesn't actually dissolve in water; rather, it sits in suspension) and served alongside tea sweets to balance out its strong taste. Perhaps because of this traditional association with sweets, today matcha is a wildly popular flavor for Japanese desserts. They do a matcha version of everything from ice creams and custards to cupcakes, cookies, macarons . . . you name it. Nestlé even sells matcha-flavored KitKats in Japan.

Like the green tea category as a whole, matcha is now widely recognized as possessing a slew of amazing health benefits. It has been credited with promoting heart health, preventing cancer, lowering cholesterol, slowing signs of aging—even helping you burn fat faster. There's been speculation that the large volumes of green tea consumed by the Japanese are linked to their incredible longevity. So, go ahead—drink up!

One final word on matcha: Keep its incredible potency in mind whenever you cook with it. I have found that unlike many types of spices and extracts, which can be added into a recipe without much adjustment, matcha is capable of altering a recipe's chemistry: a cake might rise differently or a custard fail to gel. So if you take it upon yourself to incorporate matcha into a new recipe, be aware that you may need to tinker with it a bit to get the results you want.

matcha crème brûlée

This creamy dessert is all about balance: Matcha's astringency finds its perfect complement in the sweet, creamy custard of a crème brûlée. When fashioning a hot water bath for these little puddings, be sure that you pour the water to match the level of the custard inside the cups; this will ensure that they cook evenly. The best and easiest way to create the crispy, burnt sugar crust on top of crème brûlée is with a small butane torch (which can be purchased at most kitchenware stores). If you can't get your hands on one, place the puddings directly underneath a hot broiler until the surface turns golden-brown.

SERVES 6

2 cups / 475 ml heavy whipping cream

2/3 cup / 135 g granulated sugar, plus more for sprinkling

5 teaspoons matcha powder

1 cup / 235 ml soy milk

6 large egg yolks

1. Preheat the oven to 325° F / 163°C. In a small saucepan set over medium heat, whisk together 1 cup / 235 ml of the heavy whiping cream, 1/3 cup / 66 g of the sugar, and the matcha powder; stir until the matcha and sugar are well blended. Add the remaining heavy whipping cream and the soy milk and bring the mixture to a simmer. Remove from the heat.

2. In a separate bowl, whisk together the egg yolks and the remaining sugar.

3. Whisking constantly, gradually pour the hot milk mixture into the yolk mixture. Strain through a fine mesh sieve.

4. Place 6 small (7 to 10 ounce / 198 g to 283 g) ramekins in a high-sided baking pan and divide the custard between them. Fill the baking dish with boiling water to reach most of the way up the sides of the ramekins. Carefully transfer the pan to the oven and bake for 40 to 50 minutes, or until the custard is set (it should still jiggle, but not move in liquid waves, when shaken).

5. Remove the ramekins from the water bath and chill in the refrigerator for at least 2 hours to set.

6. Before serving, remove the ramekins from the refrigerator and sprinkle each surface with a layer of sugar. Using a butane kitchen torch, melt the sugar until golden-brown all over.

FOR A GINGER VARIATION: Peel and thinly slice a 2-inch / 5 cm segment of fresh ginger and add it to the cream mixture in step 1 in place of the matcha. Once the liquid has been brought to a simmer and removed from the heat, cover and let steep for 25 minutes. Bring the liquid back to a simmer and proceed with the recipe as directed.

章 GREEN TEA

73

green tea cake *with* ginger mousse

This elegant sweet is ideal for brunches, bridal showers, or any other time when you want something light and pretty to serve to guests with tea or coffee. The ginger mousse is very delicate, so it's best to assemble the cake just before it will be eaten—especially if you're transporting it before serving.

SERVES 8

2 cups / 240 g all-purpose flour, plus more for dusting

3 tablespoons matcha, plus more for dusting

1 tablespoon baking powder

½ teaspoon salt

½ cup (1 stick) / 113 g unsalted butter, softened

¾ cup / 149 g granulated sugar

¾ cup / 164 g light brown sugar

½ teaspoon vanilla extract

3 large eggs

1 cup / 235 ml buttermilk

Ginger Mousse (recipe follows)

Confectioners' sugar, for dusting

1. Preheat the oven to 350° F / 177°C. Butter the bottoms and sides of two 8- or 9-inch / 20 or 23 cm round cake pans. Line the bottoms of the pans with parchment paper, butter the surface again, and then dust with flour, tapping out the excess.

2. In a medium bowl, whisk together the flour, matcha, baking powder, and salt.

3. In the bowl of an electric mixer fitted with a paddle attachment, beat the butter and sugars on medium-high speed until light and fluffy, 3 to 5 minutes. Beat in the vanilla extract, and then add the eggs in one at a time, scraping down the sides of the bowl as necessary.

4. Reduce the mixer speed to low. Add the flour mixture in 3 additions and the buttermilk in 2 additions, beginning and ending with the flour mixture. Mix until just combined.

5. Transfer the batter to the prepared cake pans and bake until a toothpick inserted in the center comes out clean, 25 to 30 minutes. Cool the cakes in their pans for 15 minutes, and then turn them out onto racks to cool completely.

6. Once cool, place one cake layer on a serving plate or tray. Spread a thick layer of Ginger Mousse on the surface and top it with the second cake layer. Dust the top with confectioners' sugar and matcha and serve.

ginger mousse

MAKES 3 CUPS or 710 ml

1 cup / 235 ml heavy whipping cream

1½ teaspoons freshly grated ginger

1½ teaspoons dried ginger

2 large egg whites

¼ cup / 50 g granulated sugar

3 ounces / 85 g white chocolate

1. Combine the heavy whipping cream with the fresh and dried ginger in a medium saucepan set over medium heat; bring the liquid to a simmer and simmer for 3 to 5 minutes. Cover, remove it from the heat, and refrigerate overnight. Strain the liquid through a fine mesh sieve, discarding the ginger.

2. Beat the ginger cream with an electric mixer until it forms soft peaks, and then set it aside at room temperature. In a separate bowl, whip the egg whites until soft peaks form. Gradually add the sugar and continue whipping until the peaks are firm.

3. In a double boiler set over simmering water, melt the white chocolate and then, using a whisk, fold it into the egg whites. When the whites are almost completely incorporated, fold in the whipped cream. Cover the mousse and refrigerate for about 1 hour, or until set.

japanese toast

As far as I know, French toast isn't eaten anywhere in Japan; after all, the country isn't accustomed to serving sweets at breakfast time. That didn't stop me from creating my own Japan-ified version of the iconic morning meal, by introducing matcha and soy milk into its standard egg and milk custard base. Matcha can be stubborn about blending evenly into liquid, so try using an immersion blender if it stays clumped together when whisked.

SERVES 4

1 cup / 167 g strawberries, hulled and quartered

1 tablespoon sugar

1 teaspoon lemon juice

4 large eggs

2 cups / 475 ml heavy whipping cream

2 cups / 475 ml soy milk

¼ cup / 60 ml honey

2 tablespoons matcha

1 loaf brioche, cut into twelve 1-inch slices

¼ cup (½ stick) / 57 g unsalted butter

Maple syrup, to taste

1. In a small bowl, mix together the strawberries, sugar, and lemon juice. Mash the berries firmly with the back of a spoon, and then set them aside to rest for at least 15 minutes.

2. In a large, shallow pan, whisk together the eggs, heavy whipping cream, soy milk, honey, and matcha. Working with 3 to 4 slices at a time, lay the brioche in the custard base for about 2 minutes; flip and submerge the opposite side for 2 minutes more.

3. In a large skillet set over medium heat, melt a pat of butter until it foams. Working 3 to 4 slices at a time, add the soaked brioche to the skillet, taking care not to crowd the pan. Flip the slices once they have browned on the bottom, after about 3 minutes. Cook for 3 to 4 minutes more, or until both sides are well toasted and the bread is heated through. Repeat with the remaining slices, buttering the pan between each batch. Divide between four plates and serve topped with strawberries and drizzled with maple syrup.

hojicha ice cream

Hojicha, the roasted green tea variety that has its roots in Kyoto, lends a mildly bitter, earthy flavor to this gorgeous low-fat ice cream—which is a staple at across the city's sweets shops.

MAKES 1 PINT or 475 ml

- 2 cups / 475 ml whole milk
- ½ cup / 48 g hojicha tea leaves
- 4 large egg yolks
- ⅓ cup / 66 g sugar

1. Fill a large bowl with ice and cold water and set aside.

2. Combine the milk and *hojicha* in a small saucepan over medium heat, and bring the liquid to a slow simmer, 3 to 5 minutes. Let the tea steep for 5 minutes, covered, then strain the milk mixture through a fine mesh sieve into a small bowl and discard the spent tea leaves. Wash out the saucepan and return it to the stovetop.

3. In a separate bowl, whisk together the egg yolks and the sugar. Whisking constantly, gradually pour the hot milk mixture into the yolk mixture. Pour the warmed yolk and milk mixture back into the saucepan and cook over low heat, stirring constantly with a wooden spoon or heat-resistant spatula until the custard thickens enough to coat the back of a spoon, 3 to 5 minutes.

4. Transfer the custard to a heat-resistant container set in the ice bath; stir the custard frequently until it cools to around room temperature. Cover with plastic wrap and chill thoroughly in the refrigerator.

5. Freeze the custard in an ice cream machine according to the manufacturer's instructions.

Due to its low-fat content, this ice cream is best enjoyed straight from the machine. Stored in your freezer, it loses its initial soft creaminess.

NAVIGATING THE WORLD OF JAPANESE TEA

Matcha may be the focus of this chapter, but it's just one of many tea varieties that are fundamental to Japanese cuisine—and frankly, due to its high price and strong flavor, it's probably the one that you're least likely to sip on a regular basis.

The vast majority of tea consumed in Japan is, and historically has been, green tea. But there are many different options that fall under the "green" category, varying based on qualities like the time of harvest, how much sun the leaves have seen, how the tea is processed, and what parts of the plant are used in the final product. Here's an overview of some of Japan's most popular teas, and how to brew them to the best effect (*cha* means tea in Japanese, and you can expect to see it used as a suffix with most tea varieties).

SENCHA: The most commonly consumed tea in Japan, *sencha* consists of green tea leaves that have been grown in full sunlight. Meaning simmered tea, *sencha* is delicate, mild, and slightly floral. It should be brewed for 2 minutes in simmering water (160 to 170°F / 71°C to 77°C).

GYOKURO: This high-end tea is made from first-flush green tea leaves grown partially in the shade. Sweet and mild, it should be brewed for about 3 minutes in relatively cool water (120 to 140°F / 49°C to 60°C).

BANCHA: This lower grade of *sencha* is harvested later in the year, and can include some stems in with the leaves. Its flavor is more robust and astringent than delicate *sencha*. It should be brewed for 1 to 3 minutes in simmering water (160 to 170° F / 71°C to 77°C).

HOJICHA: A reddish-brown tea made by roasting *bancha* in a clay pot over charcoal (most Japanese teas are steamed), *hojicha* is a roasty, nutty, mellow tea, low in caffeine, typically served during or after an evening meal. It should be brewed for about 1 minute in simmering water (160 to 170° F / 71°C to 77°C).

GENMAICHA: *Genmaicha* refers to any combination of dried green tea and toasted *genmai* rice grains, the latter of which provides the beverage with a nutty depth to offset the tea's natural astringency. It can be made with *sencha*, *bancha,* or *gyokuro* tea and sold premixed or created on your own at home. Brew it for 1 minute in water at a steep simmer (185° F / 85°C).

KUKICHA: Also known as twig tea, this blend of tea leaves, stems, and twigs is available as both a green tea and in roasted, oxidized form. Creamy and mild, it should be brewed for 3 minutes in simmering water (160 to 170° F / 71°C to 77°C).

MUGICHA: Not technically a tea at all, *mugicha* is made from roasted barley. This caffeine-free tisane is traditionally served cold as a summer drink in Japan; outside of Japan, it's popular as a coffee substitute. Brewing conditions needn't be as fussy for *mugicha* as for green teas, but plan to steep it for about 2 minutes in simmering water (160 to 170° F / 71°C to 77°C).

KYOTOFU

82

green tea white chocolate cupcakes

These rich, fudgy cupcakes showcase what an incredible pairing matcha and white chocolate make: the sweet, milky, salty flavor of white chocolate really mellows out matcha's tinge of bitterness.

MAKES 12 CUPCAKES

½ cup / 60 g flour

1 teaspoon baking powder

7 ounces / 198 g white chocolate

4½ ounces / 128 g (1⅛ sticks) unsalted butter

2 tablespoons shiro miso

1 cup / 115 g confectioners' sugar

3 tablespoons matcha

3 large eggs, at room temperature

1. Preheat the oven to 350° F / 177°C. In a small bowl, mix together the flour and baking powder. Set aside.

2. In a double boiler set over simmering water, melt the white chocolate, butter, and miso. Once melted and smooth, pour the mixture into the bowl of an electric mixer fitted with a paddle attachment. Add the confectioners' sugar and matcha, blending until fully incorporated.

3. Add the eggs one at a time, blending well after each addition. Add the dry ingredients gradually and mix until just combined.

4. Prepare a cupcake tin by lining the molds with foil or paper liners and divide the batter between the molds. Bake for 18 to 20 minutes, or until a cake tester or toothpick comes out clean.

matcha "rare" cheesecake

In Japan, there are two distinct styles of cheesecake: the standard oven baked variety and what they call "rare" cheesecake, a no-bake version that sets in the refrigerator with the help of gelatin. This recipe uses the latter approach, and I've made it in a variety of flavors: matcha, sweet potato, sake, passion fruit, and black sesame variations have all appeared in the Kyotofu kitchen.

MAKES 1 9-INCH or 23 cm CAKE

- 2 cups / 200 g graham cracker crumbs, from about 16 crackers
- Pinch of salt
- ½ cup (1 stick) / 113 g unsalted butter, melted and cooled slightly
- 1 tablespoon powdered gelatin
- 8 ounces / 227 g (1 package) cream cheese, at room temperature
- ¼ cup / 48 g matcha
- 1 cup / 198 g sugar
- ⅓ cup / 76 g sour cream
- 1¼ cup / 290 g silken tofu
- 1½ tablespoons shiro miso
- 2 teaspoons vanilla extract
- ½ cup / 120 ml heavy whipping cream

1. Preheat the oven to 350° F / 177°C. In the bowl of a food processor, process the graham crackers into fine crumbs. In a medium bowl, combine them with the salt and melted butter and press the mixture into the bottom of a springform pan 9 to 10 inches / 23 to 25 cm in diameter. Bake for 10 minutes and let cool to room temperature.

2. In a small bowl, sprinkle the gelatin over ¼ cup / 60 ml of cold water and let stand for 5 minutes to soften. In the bowl of an electric mixer fitted with a paddle attachment, cream the cream cheese until smooth, and then add the matcha and blend well. One at a time and blending after each addition, add the sugar, sour cream, tofu, *miso*, and vanilla extract.

3. In a small saucepan over medium heat, heat the heavy whipping cream to just below a simmer, 3 to 5 minutes. Remove from the heat and add the bloomed gelatin, whisking until no clumps remain.

4. With the mixer on low speed, add the warm cream mixture to the batter and blend until smooth.

5. Pour the cheesecake filling through a fine mesh sieve into the molded crust and cover with plastic wrap. Place in the refrigerator to chill overnight. Release the sides of the springform pan and serve.

章 GREEN TEA

頁 85

matcha ice cream

This cheerful, brightly-colored ice cream is wonderful eaten on its own or served alongside desserts like the Chocolate Tart (page 64) or Ginger "Okayu" Rice Pudding (page 125).

MAKES 1 PINT or 475 ml

- 1¼ cup / 295 ml whole milk
- ⅔ cup / 160 ml heavy whipping cream
- 2 tablespoons matcha
- ¼ cup / 50 g plus 2 tablespoons sugar, divided
- 2 large yolks
- ¼ teaspoon vanilla extract

1. Fill a large bowl with ice and cold water and set aside.

2. In a medium saucepan set over medium heat, combine the milk, cream, matcha, and ¼ cup / 50 g sugar, and bring the liquid to a simmer, about 5 minutes.

3. In a separate bowl, whisk together the egg yolks and the remaining 2 tablespoons of sugar. Whisking constantly, gradually pour about half of the hot milk mixture into the yolk mixture. Stir the warmed yolks and milk back into the saucepan and cook them over low heat, stirring constantly with a wooden spoon or heat-resistant spatula until the custard thickens enough to coat the back of a spoon, about 5 minutes. Remove the pan from the heat and stir in the vanilla extract.

4. Transfer the custard to a heat-resistant container set in the ice bath; stir the custard frequently until it cools to around room temperature. Cover with plastic wrap and chill thoroughly in the refrigerator.

5. Freeze the custard in an ice cream machine according to the manufacturer's instructions.

Due to its low-fat content, this ice cream is best enjoyed straight from the machine. Stored in your freezer, the initial soft creaminess of the custard won't last.

green tea muffins gf

One of matcha's many health benefits is that it's known to increase energy levels, so I like to work it into my morning meal whenever I can. This gently sweet breakfast treat is one of my favorite morning pick-me-ups.

MAKES 12 MUFFINS

- 1 cup / 120 g all-purpose flour
- 3 tablespoons matcha
- 1 teaspoon baking powder
- ½ teaspoon baking soda
- ¼ teaspoon salt
- 5 ounces / 142 g (1¼ sticks) unsalted butter, at room temperature
- ⅓ cup / 66 g granulated sugar
- ½ cup / 109 g packed brown sugar
- 2 large eggs
- ½ teaspoon vanilla extract
- 2 tablespoons buttermilk

1. Preheat the oven to 350° F / 177°C. Prepare a muffin tin by spraying it with nonstick cooking spray.

2. In a medium bowl, combine the flour, matcha, baking powder, baking soda, and salt.

3. In the bowl of an electric mixer fitted with a paddle attachment, cream together the butter and sugars until pale and fluffy, 3 to 5 minutes. Add the eggs, one at a time, mixing completely after each addition, followed by the vanilla extract. Add the dry ingredients slowly, alternating them with the buttermilk, and mixing until just combined.

4. Divide the batter among the 12 muffin molds and bake for 16 to 18 minutes, or until a cake tester or toothpick comes out clean. Remove from the oven and let cool to room temperature.

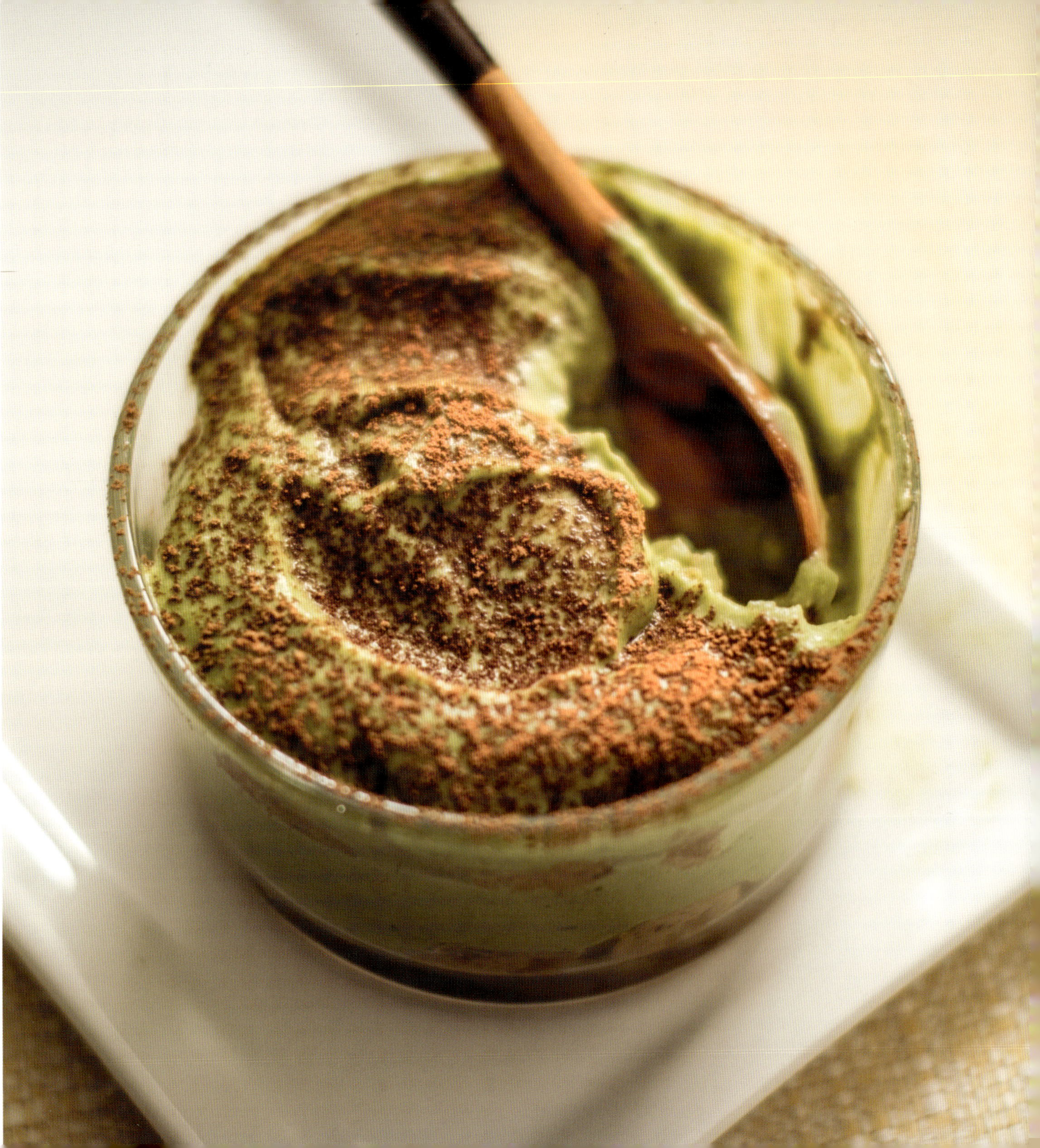

tokyo tiramisu

As with the Japanese Mont Blancs (page 48) and Matcha Crème Brûlée (page 72), tiramisu is yet another European sweet that the Japanese have taken to with gusto. This matcha-flavored twist on the Italian original is something you're likely to see in pastry cases across Japan, but with one key difference: Whereas our version includes the hint of liquor that's typical to traditional tiramisu recipes, most Japanese renditions omit the booze altogether. But I just couldn't bear to see it go.

SERVES 8

- 6 large egg yolks
- ⅓ cup / 66 g plus 2 tablespoons granulated sugar, divided
- 2 cups / 450 g mascarpone cheese
- 1 teaspoon vanilla extract
- 2 tablespoons matcha
- 1 cup / 235 ml espresso or strongly-brewed coffee
- 3 tablespoons brandy or rum
- 20 ladyfinger cookies
- Cocoa powder for dusting

1. In a double boiler set over simmering water, beat the egg yolks and ⅓ cup / 66 g sugar using a whisk or handheld electric mixer until pale yellow, thick, and tripled in volume, 5 to 8 minutes. Remove the bowl from the heat. Beat in the mascarpone, vanilla extract, and matcha.

2. In a shallow dish, stir together the hot coffee, brandy, and remaining 2 tablespoons of sugar. Dip each ladyfinger in the coffee mixture for no more than 3 seconds (letting the ladyfingers soak too long will cause them to fall apart). Place the soaked ladyfingers side by side in an 8 x 8-inch / 20 x 20 cm baking dish, breaking them in half if necessary in order to fit snuggly.

3. Spread half of the mascarpone mixture evenly over the ladyfingers. Arrange another layer of soaked ladyfingers and top with the remaining mascarpone mixture.

4. Cover the tiramisu with plastic wrap and refrigerate for at least 2 hours and up to 8 hours.

5. Sprinkle it with a dusting of cocoa powder before serving.

green tea yokan

Yokan may seem a little out of the ordinary from a Western perspective, but they are one of the most traditional sweets you'll find in Japan, a popular type of wagashi: pretty, petite treats meant to be served at a tea ceremony. The simple combination of water, sugar, matcha, and agar-agar (which functions like gelatin, but comes from seaweed) creates a jellied candy that I find to be perfect as a light midafternoon pick-me-up or a little something sweet with tea or coffee after dinner.

MAKES 32 2" x 1" or 5 cm x 2.5 cm CANDIES

4½ teaspoons agar-agar

1¾ cup / 347 g granulated sugar

3 tablespoons matcha

1. Prepare an 8 x 8-inch / 20 x 20 cm baking pan by lining it with plastic wrap. In a small saucepan set over medium-high heat, boil the agar and 2⅔ cups / 630 ml water until the mixture is clear. Reduce the liquid to a simmer.

2. In a separate bowl, whisk together the sugar and matcha, stirring until well incorporated. Add the sugar and matcha mixture to the saucepan, whisking constantly to keep the matcha from forming into clumps. Whisk until all the sugar is dissolved and the mixture is once again clear.

3. Pour the hot liquid into the baking pan, cover with plastic wrap, and let chill in the refrigerator for at least 4 hours to gel. Slice the gelled candy into 2 x 1-inch / 5 x 2.5 cm rectangles and serve them immediately, or store them refrigerated in an airtight container for up to 1 month.

章 GREEN TEA 頁

本
KYOTOFU

hoji roll cake gf

The roll cake—also known as a Swiss roll or a jellyroll—has its origins in Europe, but it has grown to become a particularly popular dessert format in Japan. This version is simply flavored with hojicha. When preparing the batter, be sure to whip the eggs and sugar until they are glossy and light as air, otherwise the finished cake is unlikely to achieve its trademark spongy, delicate consistency.

SERVES 8

- 4 large eggs, at room temperature
- ½ cup / 99 g sugar
- ½ cup / 60 g plus 2 tablespoons all-purpose flour
- ¼ ounces / 7 g hojicha tea leaves, ground to 4 teaspoons fine powder
- ¼ teaspoon baking powder
- ¼ teaspoon salt
- 1 cup / 235 ml heavy whipping cream, whipped to stiff peaks

1. Preheat the oven to 325° F / 163°C. Prepare a 13 x 8-inch / 33 x 20 cm baking sheet by lining it with parchment paper and spraying it with non-stick cooking spray.

2. In the bowl of an electric mixer fitted with the paddle attachment, blend together the eggs and the sugar on high speed until thick, glossy ribbons form, 5 to 8 minutes. Meanwhile, sift together the flour, *hojicha* powder, baking powder, and salt. Sift the mixture a second time.

3. Turn the mixer speed down to low and add the dry ingredients. Continue to mix for 30 to 45 seconds, and then turn off the mixer and finish the process by hand.

4. Spread the batter onto the prepared baking sheet in a smooth, even layer and bake for 14 minutes, rotating the pan halfway through the baking. Remove the cake from the oven.

6. Prepare a kitchen towel about 18 x 13 inches / 46 x 33 cm in size by opening it flat on the countertop and dusting it with confectioners' sugar. Loosen the edges of the cake with a knife and invert it onto the towel. Gently peel off the parchment paper. Trim ¼ inch / .5 cm of the crust off each long side of the cake. Beginning with the narrow edge, roll the cake and towel up together and let cool on a rack, seam-side down, for 10 to 15 minutes.

7. Once the cake has cooled, gently unroll it and spread the surface with whipped cream. Reroll the cake and serve immediately.

胡麻

SESAME

97	WHITE SESAME BISCOTTI
99	WHITE SESAME CAKE
100	BLACK SESAME SHORTBREAD
103	BLACK SESAME CARAMEL MOUSSE
107	BLACK SESAME & CHOCOLATE MOUSSE TARTLETS
110	BLACK SESAME "RARE" CHEESECAKE
113	BLACK SESAME MACARONS

Sesame doesn't mean much to Americans beyond the seeds we're used to seeing sprinkled atop our hamburger buns and bagels; here in the United States, they tend to serve as a decorative flourish rather than as a true flavoring agent. In Japan, the world's largest importer of sesame seeds, they are much more deeply integrated into both sweet and savory recipes.

Sesame seeds can be pressed to make a fragrant oil that stands up well to very high cooking temperatures (and works wonderfully in salad dressings); pureed into a glossy paste, a more pungent cousin to the Middle Eastern condiment tahini; and used whole, sprinkled in and on both desserts and savory dishes as a delicately crunchy, nutty garnish.

Sesame seeds are stacked with health benefits. They are full of valuable nutrients like copper, manganese, and calcium, and eating sesame seeds is thought to lower both cholesterol and blood pressure.

There a few important differences between the sesame seeds we see in America and their Japanese counterparts. First of all, in Japan the seeds are always toasted before use, which boosts their flavor in a significant way. Second, the Japanese eat not only white sesame seeds but black ones, too. This is partly for aesthetic reasons—black seeds provide a beautiful contrast when used with pale foods, whereas white seeds are preferable with dark foods—but I find that black seeds have a slightly bolder flavor, too. Lastly, I've noticed that the sesame seeds of either color that I buy from Japanese distributors have a higher oil content and are plumper than seeds from other origins, so for this reason, I try always to use Japanese brands in my cooking.

At Kyotofu, we love sesame as a way to lend a nutty flavor to sweets without resorting to peanuts; given all of the allergy issues these days, we avoid using peanuts altogether in our desserts in favor of sesame. In addition to using the seeds whole and as a paste, we also grind the seeds into sesame flour, for just one more way to incorporate them into our baked goods.

white sesame biscotti gf

The trademark Italian cookie gets a subtle Japanese tweak with the addition of white sesame seeds. Although biscotti are traditionally served with coffee, I find these to be wonderful with a cup of green tea. Don't let them rest for more than five minutes between the first and second bake, otherwise they're likely to crumble when you cut them apart.

MAKES 18 COOKIES

- ¼ cup (½ stick) / 57 g unsalted butter, melted
- 1½ tablespoons vegetable oil
- 1 large egg
- ½ cup / 99 g granulated sugar
- ¾ cup / 94 g bread flour
- ¾ cup / 83 g cake flour
- 1½ tablespoons cornmeal
- 2 tablespoons white sesame seeds, toasted
- ½ teaspoon baking powder
- ¼ teaspoon salt
- ⅓ cup / 27 g chopped roasted almonds
- 2 tablespoons chopped pistachios

1. Preheat the oven to 350° F / 177°C. Prepare a baking sheet by covering it with parchment paper or a nonstick baking mat.

2. In a small bowl, whisk together the melted butter, vegetable oil, and 1½ tablespoons of water. Whisk in the egg.

3. In medium bowl, mix together the sugar, flours, cornmeal, sesame seeds, baking powder, salt, almonds, and pistachios. Pour the butter mixture into the dry ingredients and mix to combine, using your hands to work the dough into a ball.

4. Turn the dough out onto the baking sheet and form it into a loaf about 13 inches / 33 cm long x 2½ inches / 6.5 cm wide, and ½ inch / 1 cm high.

5. Bake the biscotti loaf for 25 minutes, or until light golden-brown. Remove it from the oven and reduce the oven temperature to 325° F / 163°C.

6. Let the biscotti loaf rest for 5 minutes, and then cut the loaf horizontally, on a slight diagonal, into pieces about ½-inch / 1 cm wide. Place the individual biscotti flat on the baking sheet and return to the oven. Bake for 15 to 20 minutes, flipping the cookies halfway through, until crisp and dry. Serve warm from the oven or store in an airtight container for up to 3 weeks.

本
KYOTOFU

頁
98

white sesame cake gf

This delicate cake is a simple sweet that you can have in the oven in less than fifteen minutes, start to finish. I like to slice and serve it with tea as an afternoon snack, or pair it with fresh fruit and a scoop of Soy Milk Ice Cream (page 35) for dessert.

MAKES 1 8" x 4" or 20 cm x 10 cm LOAF

- 1 2/3 cups / 200 g all-purpose flour
- 2 teaspoons baking powder
- 1/4 teaspoon baking soda
- 1/4 teaspoon salt
- 7 1/2 ounces (1 7/8 sticks) / 213 g unsalted butter, softened
- 1/2 cup / 99 g granulated sugar
- 3/4 cup / 164 g light brown sugar
- 3 large eggs, at room temperature
- 3/4 teaspoon vanilla extract
- 3 tablespoons whole milk
- 2 tablespoons white sesame paste

1. Preheat the oven to 350° F / 177°C. Prepare an 8 x 4-inch / 20 x 10 cm loaf pan by lightly greasing it and coating it with flour.

2. In a medium bowl, mix together the flour, baking powder, baking soda, and salt.

3. In the bowl of an electric mixer fitted with a paddle attachment, cream together the butter and sugars until pale and fluffy, about 5 minutes. Add the eggs in one at a time, mixing well between each addition, and then add the vanilla extract.

4. Add the dry ingredients in 3 additions, alternating with a tablespoon of the milk in between. Add the white sesame paste, mixing until well incorporated.

5. Scrape the batter into the loaf pan and bake it for 40 to 45 minutes, or until a cake tester comes out clean; rotate the pan halfway through baking.

black sesame shortbread

This recipe yields a big batch of shortbread—three dozen cookies, or up to four dozen if you decide to gather and reroll the dough scraps after stamping out your first round of cookies—but since it contains just a single egg, I don't like to scale down its size any further. Regardless, these never go to waste in my house. They make excellent gifts (especially around the holidays), and keep for weeks and weeks in an airtight container.

MAKES 3 to 4 DOZEN COOKIES

- 2⅓ cups / 280 g all-purpose flour
- ½ cup / 71 g toasted black sesame seeds, ground to a fine flour in a spice grinder
- ¾ teaspoons baking powder
- ¼ teaspoons salt
- ½ cup (1 stick) / 113 g unsalted butter, softened
- 1 cup / 198 g granulated sugar
- 1 large egg
- 1 tablespoon whole milk

1. In a medium bowl, combine the all-purpose flour, sesame flour, baking powder, and salt.

2. In the bowl of an electric mixer fitted with a paddle attachment, cream together the butter and sugar until pale and fluffy, 3 to 5 minutes. Add the egg and milk, scraping down the sides of bowl after blending.

3. Gradually add the dry ingredients into the creamed butter, mixing just until the dough comes together. Remove the dough from the mixer; use a spatula or bowl scraper to mix in by hand any dry ingredients left at bottom of the bowl. Pat the dough into two disks, wrap them in plastic wrap, and let them chill in the refrigerator for at least 30 minutes.

4. Preheat the oven to 350° F / 177°C and position one of the oven racks a third of the way from the top of the oven. Prepare two baking sheets by lining them with parchment paper. On a floured work surface, roll one of the disks out ¼-inch / .5 cm thick and stamp out cookies using a 2-inch / 5 cm round cutter. Gather up the dough scraps, reroll them, and stamp out more cookies, if desired. Place the cookies on the two baking sheets and chill in the refrigerator for 15 minutes. Repeat the process with the second disk of dough.

5. Bake the cookies on the top oven rack for 12 minutes, or until light golden-brown, rotating the pans halfway through baking. Let cool on a wire rack and serve immediately, or store in an airtight container for up to 3 weeks.

FOR A WHITE SESAME VARIATION: Substitute the black sesame seeds for an equal amount of toasted white sesame seeds.

FOR A MATCHA VARIATION: Substitute the black sesame flour for 3 tablespoons matcha powder.

FOR A HOJICHA VARIATION: Substitute the black sesame flour for ¼ cup / 24 g hojicha tea leaves, ground to a fine powder in a spice grinder.

FOR A YUZU VARIATION: Omit the black sesame flour and substitute 1 tablespoon yuzu juice for the whole milk.

FOR A GENMAI VARIATION: Substitute the black sesame flour for ¼ cup / 32 g genmai powder, ground in a spice grinder from about ⅓ cup / 70 g iri genmai grains, plus 2 teaspoons whole iri genmai.

章 SESAME

本 KYOTOFU

black sesame caramel mousse

The difference between a great mousse and a good one all comes down to texture. The key to achieving the lightest and most delicate results lie in the combination of eggs and sugar. Be sure to whip your eggs yolks thoroughly, and after adding the hot sugar syrup, don't be afraid to keep whisking the mixture until it grows noticeably in volume, transforming from a liquid to glossy, opaque ribbons.

SERVES 6

¼ cup / 50 g sugar

2 tablespoons boiling water

3 large egg yolks

1 ¼ cups / 288 g whipped cream, from about ¾ cups / 180 ml heavy whipping cream

¼ cup / 75 g Caramel (recipe follows)

2 tablespoons toasted black sesame seeds

Black Sesame Tuile (page 167)

1. In a medium saucepan fitted with a candy thermometer, combine the sugar with the boiling water and stir to combine. Once the sugar is fully dissolved, bring the mixture to a boil over medium heat.

2. Meanwhile, in the bowl of an electric mixer fitted with a whisk attachment, whisk the egg yolks until pale and creamy. When the sugar syrup has reached 248° F / 120°C or it can be formed into a soft ball in cold water, remove it from the heat immediately and, with the mixer running, drizzle the syrup onto the yolks. Beat at high speed for 3 to 5 minutes, or until the mixture evolves into a firm, yellow foam. Turn off the mixer and let the mixture cool to room temperature, whisking from time to time.

3. Fold in the whipped cream, Caramel, and black sesame seeds. Cover with plastic wrap and chill in the refrigerator for at least 2 hours. Scoop into individual bowls or cups and serve chilled, garnished with a Black Sesame Tuile, if desired.

caramel

MAKES 1 CUP or 300 g

½ cup / 99 g sugar

¼ cup / 60 ml corn syrup

½ cup 120 ml heavy whipping cream

2¼ ounces / 64 g unsalted butter, softened and cubed

1. In a heavy-bottomed medium saucepan over medium-high heat, stir together the sugar, corn syrup, and 4 tablespoons of water to completely moisten the sugar. Heat, stirring constantly, until the sugar dissolves and the syrup begins to bubble. Stop stirring and allow the mixture to boil undisturbed until it turns a medium amber color.

2. Immediately remove the caramel from the heat and slowly pour the heavy whipping cream into the caramel (it will bubble madly). Use a wooden spoon to stir the mixture until completely smooth. If any lumps remain, return the pan to the heat and stir until dissolved. Whisk in the butter. Allow the sauce to cool slightly, then use immediately or store in the refrigerator for up to 1 week, heating before use.

THE WAY OF TEA

The history of sweets in Japan is inextricably linked to the tea ceremony. Or, as it's known in Japanese, chanoyu: "the way of tea."

The tea ceremony in its current form dates back to the sixteenth century, when Zen masters codified this particular ritual as a means of focusing the senses on the beauty of the here and now. A tea ceremony isn't simply about eating and drinking. It's a forum for social connection, philosophical contemplation, and elevated conversation, as well as an artistic performance in its own right; the host's every gesture is choreographed and rehearsed, and every aesthetic detail is painstakingly chosen.

The specifics of the tea ceremony vary greatly by season, location, time of day, and level of formality, but the central idea always revolves around preparing and drinking green tea in an intimate setting—typically, a purpose-built tea room or tea house—with a small group of invited guests.

At the heart of the tea ceremony is matcha. The host takes great care in selecting particular tea tools for the occasion, cleaning them meticulously in the front of his or her guests, and arranging them in a specific fashion. He or she then ritually whips matcha into hot water using a wooden whisk to make a strong, bitter drink. Small, delicate *wagashi*—or tea sweets—are served along with the tea to balance out its bitterness. The combination of bitter and sweet is not only pleasing to the senses, but symbolic of the balance that's central to the Japanese outlook on life.

Although formal tea ceremonies are becoming less and less common today, Japanese people of all ages still take tea classes and belong to tea clubs where they practice the finer points of the ceremony ritual from the perspective of both host and guest. It can take years of study to achieve mastery of this uniquely Japanese art form.

本
KYOTOFU

black sesame & chocolate mousse tartlets gf

These individually portioned tarts are a bit of a labor of love, but their deep chocolate flavor and elegant appearance always make a big impression. I find them to be a wonderful make-ahead dessert when hosting guests for dinner; the tartlets can be stored in the freezer for up to a week, and then quickly glazed before serving.

SERVES 8

½ cup (1 stick) / 113 g unsalted butter, softened

½ cup / 58 g plus 2 tablespoons confectioners' sugar

1 large egg

1 cup / 125 g plus 2 tablespoons bread flour

¼ cup / 35 g toasted black sesame seeds, ground to a fine flour in a spice grinder

2 tablespoons cornstarch

¼ teaspoon salt

Chocolate Mousse (recipe follows)

Chocolate Glaze (recipe follows)

1. In the bowl of an electric mixer fitted with a paddle attachment, beat the butter and sugar until light and fluffy, 3 to 5 minutes. Add the egg and beat until well combined. In a separate bowl, whisk together the bread flour, sesame flour, cornstarch, and salt.

2. Add the flour mixture to the mixer bowl and beat until just incorporated, taking care not to over mix the dough.

3. Transfer the dough to a lightly floured work surface and knead it a few times to bring it together. Wrap the dough in plastic wrap and refrigerate until firm, at least 1 hour.

4. Preheat the oven to 350° F / 177°C. On a lightly floured work surface, roll the dough out to a ¼-inch / .5 cm thickness and stamp out rounds using a 3-inch / 7.5 cm round cutter, rerolling the scraps if necessary to yield 8 in total.

5. Bake the rounds for 18 to 20 minutes, or until golden-brown around the edges. Remove from the oven and let cool to room temperature.

6. Spoon the Chocolate Mousse into a pastry bag fitted with a ½-inch / 1 cm star tip. Pipe the mousse on top of each pastry round in concentric circles, such that you create a decorative crown of mousse. Place the tarts in the freezer and allow them to chill for at least 2 hours, or until the mousse is firm.

7. Before serving, remove the tarts from the freezer and drizzle each with warm Chocolate Glaze.

chocolate mousse

SERVES 8

- 2 egg whites
- 1½ tablespoons granulated sugar
- 1¼ cups / 295 ml heavy whipping cream
- 1½ teaspoons powdered gelatin
- ⅓ cup / 80 ml whole milk
- 2 large eggs
- 10 ounces / 283 g milk chocolate, chopped

1. In a medium bowl, whip the egg whites to soft peaks, add the sugar, and continue to beat until stiff and glossy. In a separate medium bowl, whip the cream into stiff peaks. Set both bowls aside.

2. In a small bowl, sprinkle the gelatin over ¼ cup / 60 ml of cold water and let stand for 5 minutes to soften.

3. In a small saucepan set over medium heat, whisk the bloomed gelatin into the milk, taking care to break up any lumps. Bring the mixture to a boil, and remove the pan from the heat.

4. In a double boiler set over simmering water, beat the eggs using a whisk or handheld electric mixer until pale yellow, thick, and tripled in volume, 5 to 8 minutes. Meanwhile, place the chocolate in a glass bowl and microwave it in 30 second increments, stirring between each session until completely melted and smooth.

5. Remove the eggs from the heat and add the melted chocolate in a slow stream, stirring constantly to ensure the eggs don't curdle. Once the chocolate is incorporated, stir in the milk and gelatin mixture. Fold in the egg whites, followed by the whipped cream. Cover the mousse with plastic wrap and refrigerate for at least 2 hours, or until set.

chocolate glaze

MAKES 1 CUP or 235 ml

3½ ounces / 99 g dark chocolate, chopped (64% cacao)

1 tablespoon vegetable oil

1 tablespoon plus 1 teaspoon light corn syrup

½ teaspoon powdered gelatin

½ cup plus 2 tablespoons heavy whipping cream

2 tablespoons granulated sugar

2½ tablespoons unsweetened black cocoa powder (substitute standard unsweetened cocoa)

1. In a double boiler set over simmering water, melt together the chocolate, vegetable oil, and corn syrup.

2. In a small bowl, sprinkle the gelatin over 2 tablespoons of cold water and let stand for 5 minutes to soften. In a small saucepan, bring 1½ teaspoons of water, the cream, and the sugar to a simmer. Remove the pan from the heat and whisk in the gelatin until it's fully dissolved. Whisk in the cocoa and melted chocolate mixture until smooth and glossy.

3. Strain the glaze through a fine mesh sieve into a glass bowl (metal will affect the taste). Let cool slightly and use immediately, or store in the refrigerator and reheat in the microwave before use.

black sesame "rare" cheesecake

When tasting this spectacular cheesecake for the first time, many of our customers describe it as being somehow both intensely unique and strangely familiar. I suspect that's because while most Americans have never tasted the flavor of black sesame in a soft, creamy format like a cheesecake, the ingredient combination does have precedent here—think sesame bagels with creamed cheese.

MAKES 1 9" or 23 cm CHEESECAKE

- 2 cups / 200 g graham cracker crumbs, from about 16 crackers
- Pinch of salt
- ¾ cup (1¼ sticks) / 170 g unsalted butter, melted and cooled slightly
- ¼ cup / 56 g white sesame paste
- 1 tablespoon powdered gelatin
- 8 ounces / 227 g (1 package) cream cheese, at room temperature
- ¼ cup / 56 g black sesame paste
- 1 cup / 198 g granulated sugar
- ⅓ cup / 76 g sour cream
- 1 cup / 232 g silken tofu
- 1½ tablespoons shiro miso
- 2 teaspoons vanilla extract
- ½ cup / 120 ml heavy whipping cream

1. Preheat the oven to 350° F / 177°C. In the bowl of a food processor, process the graham crackers into fine crumbs. In a medium bowl, combine the crumbs with the salt, melted butter, and white sesame paste, and press the mixture into the bottom of a springform pan 9 to 10 inches / 23 to 25 cm in diameter. Bake for 10 minutes and let cool to room temperature.

2. In a small bowl, sprinkle the gelatin over ¼ cup / 60 ml of cold water and let stand for 5 minutes to soften. In the bowl of an electric mixer fitted with a paddle attachment, cream the cream cheese until smooth, and then add the black sesame paste and blend well. One at a time and blending after each addition, add the sugar, sour cream, tofu, miso, and vanilla extract.

3. In a small saucepan over medium heat, heat the heavy whipping cream to just below a simmer, 3 to 5 minutes. Remove from the heat and add the bloomed gelatin, whisking until no clumps remain.

4. With the mixer on low speed, add in the warm cream mixture to the batter and blend until smooth.

5. Pour the cheesecake filling through a fine mesh sieve into the molded crust and cover with plastic wrap. Place in the refrigerator to chill overnight. Release the sides of the springform pan and serve.

章 SESAME

頁 111

本
KYOTOFU

black sesame macarons

The Japanese have fallen for French macarons in a big way, and it's not hard to see why they're as readily available today in Tokyo as they are in Paris: Light as air, petite, and painstakingly crafted, macarons embody so many of the attributes that the Japanese have traditionally valued in their sweets. I love black sesame as a slightly off-beat flavor; something a little different from the standard-issue chocolate, hazelnut, and raspberry that you find all around the world. Macarons are notoriously finicky to make, so be sure to follow the recipe as precisely as possible for cookies that are maximally light and tender.

MAKES 12 COOKIES

2 egg whites, divided

½ cup / 99 g granulated sugar

1 cup / 115 g confectioners' sugar

1 cup / 112 g almond flour

1 tablespoon black sesame paste

Black Sesame Filling (recipe follows)

1. Preheat the oven to 350° F / 177°C. Prepare two baking sheets by lining them with parchment paper.

2. In the bowl of an electric mixer fitted with a whisk attachment, or using a handheld electric mixer, whisk 1 egg white on medium-low speed until foamy. Increase the speed to medium and whisk the egg white until soft peaks form.

3. Meanwhile, in a small saucepan fitted with a candy thermometer and set over medium-high heat, combine the granulated sugar with 2½ tablespoons of water and bring it to a boil, stirring and swirling the pan from time to time until the sugar dissolves. Cook, undisturbed, until the syrup registers 250° F / 121°C or it can be formed into a soft ball in cold water.

4. Reduce the mixer speed to low and immediately pour the hot sugar syrup down the side of the mixer bowl in a slow, steady stream, incorporating it into the whipped egg white. Increase the speed to high, and beat until the mixture is thick and glossy, about 3 minutes.

5. Sift together the confectioners' sugar and almond flour, then sift them a second time. Add the flour mixture to the bowl of a food processor. In a separate bowl, mix together the remaining egg white and the black sesame paste. Add the black sesame mixture to the flour mixture in the food processor, pulsing to combine until the mixture resembles a course meal. Transfer the mixture to a large bowl and fold in the whipped meringue.

(continued on next page)

(continued from previous page)

6 | Scoop the macaron batter in a piping bag fitted with a 1/2-inch / 1 cm round tip. Pipe 12 circles about 1 1/2 inches / 4 cm in diameter onto each baking sheet, tapping the tray on the counter to remove any air bubbles. Let rest for 20 to 30 minutes, or until the cookies' surfaces are no longer tacky.

7 | Bake the macarons for 6 minutes. Without opening the oven door, turn off the heat and let bake for an additional 5 minutes. Remove the macarons from the oven and let cool to room temperature.

8 | Once cool, sandwich the macarons with Black Sesame Filling and serve.

FOR A MATCHA VARIATION: Omit the black sesame paste and sift 2 teaspoons of matcha in with the dry ingredients.

black sesame filling

MAKES 3/4 CUP or 180 ml

- 3½ ounces (⅞ stick) / 99 g unsalted butter, softened
- 2 large egg yolks
- ¼ cup / 50 g granulated sugar
- 3½ tablespoons whole milk
- 1 teaspoon vanilla extract
- 1 teaspoon black sesame paste

1. Cut the butter into small pieces, place them in a small bowl, and mash with a spatula or wooden spoon until smooth and creamy.

2. In a small bowl, whisk together the egg yolks and sugar until the mixture is pale yellow and the sugar is fully dissolved. Whisk in the milk.

3. Pour the egg mixture into a small saucepan over low heat, whisking constantly to ensure that the mixture does not curdle or scorch. Cook until the mixture becomes thick and custardy, about the consistency of pudding, 7 to 10 minutes.

4. Pour the egg mixture back into its bowl, whisking until it's no warmer than room temperature. Whisk in the butter in three batches; if the egg custard is warm, the butter will melt and ruin the consistency. Add the vanilla extract and black sesame paste and stir until all of the ingredients are fully combined.

FOR A MATCHA VARIATION: Whisk 1 teaspoon matcha in with the eggs and sugar. Omit the black sesame paste.

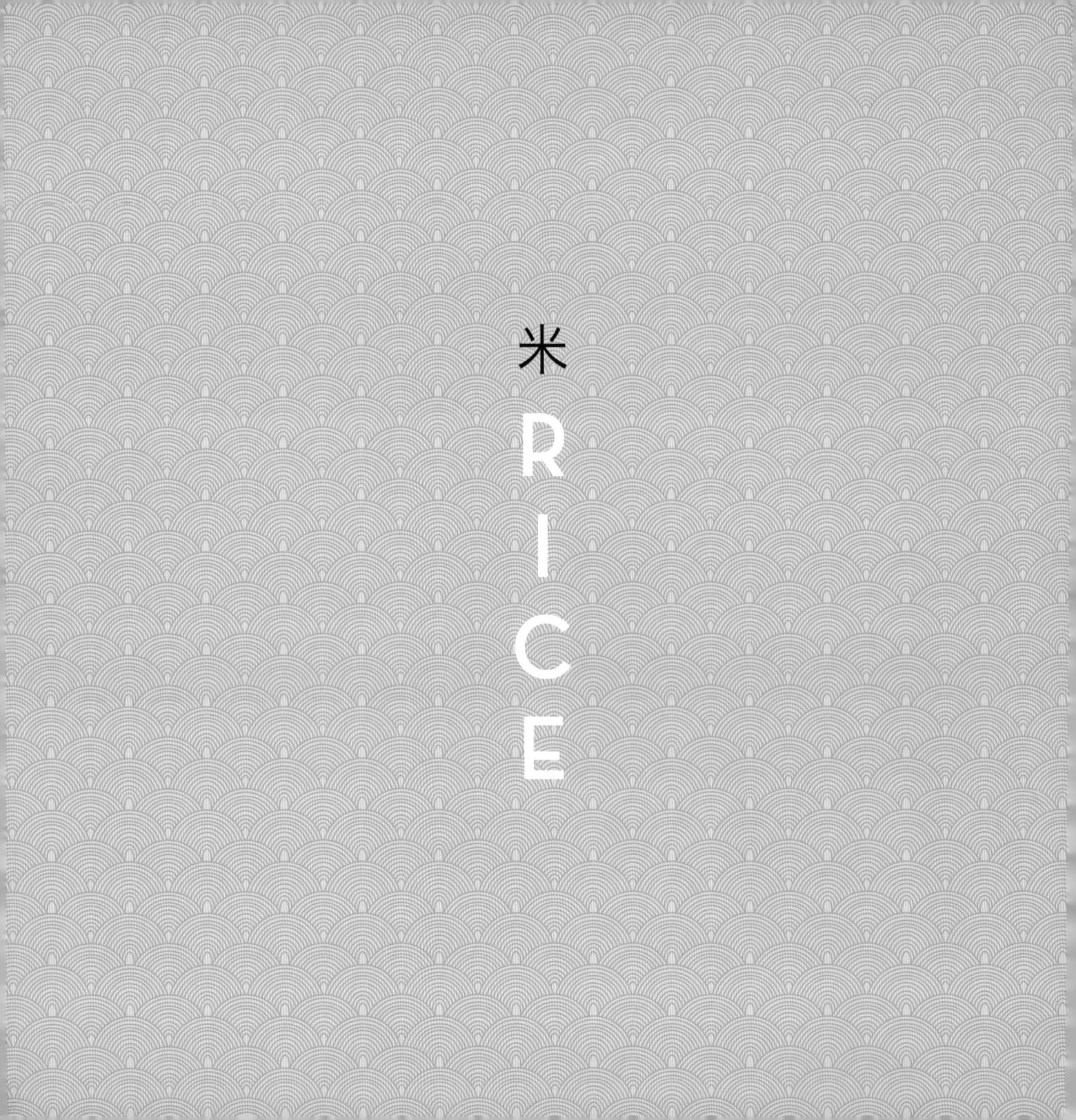

米

RICE

119	BROWN RICE MADELEINES
120	BROWN RICE FINANCIERS
122	MISO MOCHI
125	GINGER "OKAYU" RICE PUDDING
126	BROWN RICE "NAMA" CHOCOLATES
128	PASSION FRUIT MOCHI ICE CREAM
131	DAIFUKU

No book of Japanese recipes, desserts, or otherwise, would be complete without a few words about rice. It is the most basic element of the Japanese diet, eaten at every meal (including breakfast), whether on its own are as an ingredient in a larger dish.

Given the important place that rice occupies in Japanese culinary life, there are a few different ways that I've thought to incorporate it into Kyotofu's desserts.

The first, and most conventional, is with mochi. Mochi is a chewy, sweet rice dough that plays a traditional role in Japanese confectionary. The old-fashioned way to make it is to soak and cook special glutinous rice—don't worry, it doesn't contain gluten!—and then pound it with heavy mallets into a gummy dough (an amusing aside: Where Americans see "the man in the moon," the Japanese see a rabbit pounding mochi on the lunar surface). The shortcut method, which is what I describe in this book, is to add water to *shiratamako* or mochiko, rice flours made from grinding up cooked glutinous rice, and then cook the dough in a frying pan until thickened.

Mochi can be flavored with all kinds of fruit purees, or simply sweetened with sugar. It can be chilled, cut into pieces, and baked into cupcakes; cut into squares and served as a petit four with tea; formed into balls and boiled; rolled flat and filled with red bean paste, or, as is more popular here in America, with ice cream.

Another way that I like to incorporate rice into Kyotofu's desserts is with *iri genmai*. *Iri genmai* is roasted brown rice that is sometimes added to green tea for a nutty, toasty flavor component. I buy *iri genmai* on its own, grind it coarsely in a spice grinder, and add it to cookies and cakes. A little bit mixed into batters and doughs adds a wonderful crunchy texture and roasted flavor.

So-called "ordinary" rice—what we in the West refer to as sushi rice—isn't typically found in Japanese sweets either, but I manage to work with it in one instance: I make a sweet version of *okayu*, a traditional porridge dish, which works out to be something of a Japanese take on rice pudding. Once you try rice pudding made with Japan's sticky, short-grained rice, you'll never go back to American rice varieties!

brown rice madeleines

Iri genmai is used strictly as a tea component in Japan, but I love the crunchy texture and toasty flavor that this roasted rice contributes when it's coarsely ground and added into baked goods. When making these madeleines—the very traditional French cookies that have gained popularity in Japan—be careful not to over bake them, as they will lose their soft, springy texture after even a little too much time in the oven.

MAKES ABOUT 16 COOKIES

- ½ cup / 105 g iri genmai
- 2 large eggs
- ½ cup / 99 g granulated sugar
- Zest of 1 lemon
- 3½ ounces / 99 g (⅞ stick) unsalted butter, melted
- 4 teaspoons vegetable oil
- ⅓ cup / 42 g bread flour
- ⅓ cup / 37 g cake flour
- ¼ teaspoon baking powder
- ¼ teaspoon salt

1. In a spice grinder or food processor, coarsely grind the *iri genmai* into chunky bits slightly larger than a pearl of couscous.

2. In a medium bowl, whisk together the eggs, sugar, lemon zest, butter, and vegetable oil. In a separate bowl, combine the ground *iri genmai*, flours, baking powder, and salt. Add the dry ingredients to the wet ingredients and mix until just combined. Cover the bowl with plastic wrap and refrigerate overnight.

3. Preheat the oven to 350° F / 177°C. Prepare a madeleine pan by spraying it with nonstick cooking spray. Place a tablespoon-sized ball of batter in the center of each mold (do not spread the batter out). Bake the cookies for 7 minutes, rotate the pan halfway, and bake for 5 minutes more, or until the surface of the madeleines spring back when touched. Remove from the oven and serve immediately.

These baking times are based on using a metal madeleine pan. If you are using a silicone pan, increase the baking time by 4 to 6 minutes.

brown rice financiers gf

Financiers, those little almond cakes from Paris, are traditionally made in rectangular molds of varying sizes; their shape is said to mimic bars of gold. But this tender dough can be baked in any number of shapes. We tend to make them in flower molds at Kyotofu, and an oblong boat shape is a popular choice for many bakeries. If you don't have the time or inclination to buy specialty molds, you can also make round financiers in mini- or standard-sized muffin tins. If you alter the size of the mold so that you're using more batter per financier, just be sure to adjust the baking time accordingly. Remove these little tea cakes from the oven as soon as they are light golden in color and spring back to the touch.

MAKES 20 4" x 2" or 5 cm x 10 cm COOKIES

- ½ cup / 55 g cake flour
- ¾ cup / 84 g almond flour
- Pinch salt
- 1 cup (2 sticks) / 227 g unsalted butter
- 6 large egg whites
- 2 cups / 230 g confectioners' sugar
- ¼ cup / 53 g iri genmai, processed to nubs in a spice grinder

1. Preheat the oven to 350° F / 177°C. Prepare financier molds by greasing them with butter.

2. In a medium bowl, combine the cake flour, almond flour, and salt. Meanwhile, in a small saucepan set over medium heat, melt the butter and let it continue to cook until it reaches a medium brown color. Immediately remove from the heat and let cool to room temperature.

3. In a medium bowl, combine the egg whites and confectioners' sugar and whisk until slightly frothy. Add the dry ingredients in three additions, alternating with the brown butter, beginning and ending with the dry ingredients. Stir in the *iri genmai* until just combined.

4. Spoon the batter to fill the *financier* molds and bake them for 7 minutes, turn the pan halfway, then bake them for 7 minutes more, or until they are a light golden color. Remove from the oven and let cool before unmolding.

FOR A MATCHA VARIATION: Substitute the *iri genmai* for 2 tablespoons matcha.

章 RICE

頁

121

miso mochi

Rather than using mochi as a wrapper, here the gummy rice dough becomes a candy of sorts, flavored simply with sweet saikyo miso. A dough made with mochiko like this one tends to harden after a couple of days, so plan to serve these mochi cubes within a day or so of making them.

MAKES 32 1" CUBES

- 1 cup / 204 g mochiko
- ½ teaspoon saikyo miso
- ¼ cup / 50 g sugar
- ⅓ cup / 80 ml hot water
- Cornstarch, for dusting

1. In a medium bowl, combine the mochiko and ⅓ cup / 80 ml water and knead the mixture with your hands until smooth.

2. In a separate bowl, dissolve the *saikyo miso* and sugar in the hot (about 180°F / 82°C) water, whisking to make sure the *miso* and sugar are fully dissolved. Add this to the mochi dough and stir until combined.

3. In a nonstick pan set over medium-high heat, cook the dough; stir constantly using a rubber spatula. Cook until the mochi becomes very thick and slightly translucent, about 5 minutes.

4. Dust an 8 x 4-inch / 20 x 10 cm pan with cornstarch. Scrape the mochi into the pan and spread it in an even layer about 1-inch / 2.5 cm thick. Dust the top with cornstarch, cover with plastic wrap, and chill in the refrigerator for 1 hour or longer. Cut the mochi into 1-inch / 2.5 cm cubes and serve.

THE ART OF WAGASHI

To talk about traditional Japanese sweets is to talk about *wagashi*, the artful, intricately crafted morsels customarily served with tea. Until the mid-1800s, when European and American confections came flooding into a Japan newly open to trade, these so-called "tea sweets" were the closest thing the Japanese had to a Western-style concept of dessert.

Wagashi date back to the seventh century, when they emerged as an art form in the imperial capital of Kyoto (*gashi* means confections and *wa* denotes all things Japanese). Over the course of the coming centuries, their evolution was influenced by confectionary introduced from China, and later, Portugal and Spain.

Bite-sized *wagashi* are most commonly made from sweetened white and red azuki bean paste, agar-agar, rice flour, and a very precious, high-end sugar called *wasambonto*. There are numerous varieties, many of which are inspired by nature and meant to vary with the seasons. There are specific *wagashi* for particular festivals, and ones to mark life's milestones. As is the case with luxury chocolates in Western culture, *wagashi* are less commonly made in the home than purchased as gifts from high-end shops and department stores.

Some common forms of *wagashi* are yokan (page 90), the little jellied rectangles flavored with azuki bean paste or matcha; *monaka*, which consists of azuki bean paste sandwiched in between two decorative rice wafers; and *higashi*, a dried confection made of rice flour and sugar molded into beautiful designs.

Although *wagashi* are strictly a special-occasion sweet in Japan, I view the philosophy behind them as something that we all can apply to anything we cook or eat. *Wagashi* are intended to be a pleasure to *all five* senses. Their physical beauty, invoking nature, the seasons, and landscapes, should appeal to the eyes; varying textures are meant as a pleasure to touch; lovely aromas enchant our sense of smell; poetic, lyrical names please our ears; and of course, their beautiful flavors appeal to our taste buds. It's an idea that inspires me every time I step in the kitchen.

KYOTOFU

ginger "okayu" rice pudding

The Japanese don't have an exact rice pudding equivalent in their traditional cuisine, which is a little bit surprising given their deep love for puddings in general, and the prominence of rice in their diet. What they do have is okayu, a savory, congee-like rice porridge dish that's the closest thing in Japanese cuisine to comfort food. In the spirit of innovation, we have dubbed this dish "okayu" rice pudding and we make it using Japanese sushi rice and soy milk. This version is flavored with ginger, a favorite wintertime spice in Japan.

SERVES 6

- 2 tablespoons freshly grated ginger root, from a 4-inch / 10 cm knob of ginger
- 2 cups / 475 ml whole milk
- 1½ cups / 355 ml soy milk
- ½ cup / 138 g Japanese sushi rice
- ¼ cup / 50 g granulated sugar
- 1 tablespoon Kuromitsu Syrup (page 169), or blackstrap molasses
- ½ cup / 120 ml heavy whipping cream
- Ginger Syrup (page 166)

1. Wrap the freshly grated ginger in cheesecloth and tie it off with twine. In a large saucepan over medium heat, combine the milk, soy milk, and the grated ginger sachet. Cover the saucepan and bring it to a simmer; allow the ginger to infuse the milk for 15 to 20 minutes.

2. Stir the rice, sugar, and Kuromitsu Syrup into the pan; increase the heat to high. Once the mixture has come to a boil, reduce the heat to medium-low and gently simmer uncovered, stirring frequently, for 30 to 35 minutes. Once the pudding is thick and the rice is tender, pour in the heavy whipping cream.

3. Remove and discard the ginger sachet and serve the rice pudding, while still warm, with a little Ginger Syrup drizzled over the top of each bowl.

FOR A PERSIMMON VARIATION: In step 1, omit the freshly grated ginger. In a large saucepan over medium heat, combine 1 cup / 235 ml water with ½ cup / 99 g sugar and 2 medium-sized, ripe, peeled and diced Fuyu persimmons and bring the mixture to a boil. Cook until the persimmons are very soft, about 10 minutes, and puree the mixture using an immersion blender. Add the milk and soy milk and continue with the recipe, starting from step 2. Omit the ginger syrup.

brown rice "nama" chocolates

The Japanese answer to American fudge or French truffles, so-called Nama Chocolates were invented in the 1990s by the high-end Japanese confectionary brand Royce'. The silken, tender chocolate squares have since become a well-loved luxury sweet across Japan, and we make our own versions in homage with flavorings like genmai, hojicha, and matcha. Due to the inclusion of fresh dairy, these chocolates must be refrigerated at all times and are best consumed within a few days.

MAKES 16 2" or 5 cm SQUARES

- 12 ounces / 340 g white chocolate, coarsely chopped
- ½ cup / 120 ml heavy whipping cream
- 3 tablespoons *iri genmai*, coarsely ground in a spice grinder

1. Place the white chocolate in a medium bowl and set aside.

2. In a small saucepan set over medium-high heat, whisk together the heavy whipping cream and *genmai* bits, stirring frequently. Once the mixture begins to boil, after about 5 minutes, pour the cream mixture over the white chocolate and let it sit for 1 minute. Stir the mixture with a wooden spoon or spatula until the chocolate is completely melted and incorporated with the cream.

3. Pour the mixture into an 8 x 8-inch / 20 x 20 cm baking dish. Tap the baking dish on the counter to move any air bubbles to the surface; pop stubborn ones using a toothpick. Cover with plastic wrap and chill in the refrigerator until set, at least 4 hours. Once hardened, cut the chocolate into 2-inch / 5 cm squares and serve.

FOR A MATCHA VARIATION: Substitute 2 tablespoons matcha for the *iri genmai* bits.

FOR HOJICHA VARIATION: Substitute 2 tablespoons finely ground *hojicha* for the *iri genmai* bits.

章 RICE

頁

127

passion fruit mochi ice cream

If you came to this book familiar with just one Japanese dessert, it was probably mochi ice cream, a common after-dinner sweet served at American sushi restaurants. This spin on traditional Japanese daifuku—red bean paste wrapped in mochi—actually has its roots in Los Angeles, where it was first invented in the early 90s by a company called Mikawaya. Mochi ice cream has since spread back to Japan and has become a popular dessert there in its own right. While the recipe below is for a passion fruit version (my personal favorite), you can make it in a wide range of different flavors by simply substituting equal quantities of a different fruit puree. Think peach, raspberry, persimmon, or apricot.

MAKES 12 1.5" or 4 cm DUMPLINGS

½ cup / 60 g plus 1 tablespoon shiratamako

3 tablespoons passion fruit pulp, from 3 small or 2 large ripe fruits

¾ cup / 149 g granulated sugar

Corn starch, for dusting

Passion Fruit Ice Cream (recipe follows)

1. In a medium bowl, combine the *shiratamako* with ¼ cup / 60 ml of water. Using your hands, knead the mixture until smooth.

2. In a separate bowl, dilute the passion fruit pulp with 2 tablespoons of water. Add this to the mochi dough and stir until combined. Stir in the sugar.

3. Dust a small bowl with cornstarch. In a medium nonstick pan over medium heat, cook the mochi dough; stir constantly using a rubber spatula. Cook until the mochi becomes very thick, slightly translucent, and hangs together as a dough, about 5 minutes. Remove it to the bowl, sprinkle the surface generously with cornstarch, and cover with plastic wrap. Place in the refrigerator for 30 minutes to chill.

4. Dust a cutting board heavily with cornstarch; prepare a baking sheet by lining it with parchment paper and placing it in the freezer to chill. With cornstarch-dusted fingers, pinch off a generous tablespoon of chilled mochi—it will be very sticky—and place it on the cutting board. Using a rolling pin coated in cornstarch, roll the mochi into a 3-inch / 7.5 cm round about ⅛-inch / .3 cm thick. Place the finished mochi wrapper on the baking sheet and leave the baking sheet in the freezer to chill as you roll the remaining wrappers.

5. Remove the mochi wrappers from the freezer. Working one at a time, fill each with a tablespoon-sized ball of ice cream. Gather the mochi around the ice cream, pinching off the edges at the top to form a sealed ball. Place the ball seam-side down on the baking sheet and store in the freezer until ready to use.

passion fruit ice cream

MAKES 1 PINT or 475 ml

4 large egg yolks

⅓ cup / 66 g granulated sugar

1⅓ cups / 315 ml heavy whipping cream

⅔ cup / 145 g passion fruit pulp, from 14 small or 8 large ripe fruits

1. Fill a large bowl with ice and cold water and set aside.

2. In a medium bowl, whisk together the egg yolks and the sugar. Meanwhile, in a small saucepan, heat the cream just until it begins to boil. Whisking constantly, gradually pour about half of the hot milk mixture into the yolk mixture. Stir the warmed yolk and milk mixture back into the saucepan and cook over low heat, stirring constantly with a wooden spoon or heat-resistant spatula until the custard thickens enough to coat the back of a spoon, 3 to 5 minutes.

3. Transfer the custard to a heat-resistant container set in the ice bath; stir the custard frequently until it cools to around room temperature. Cover with plastic wrap and chill thoroughly in the refrigerator.

4. Freeze the custard in an ice cream machine according to the manufacturer's instructions.

本
KYOTOFU

daifuku

A traditional tea sweet, daifuku means "great luck" in Japanese. These little dumplings are ubiquitous in Japan, sold as desserts or snacks everywhere from high-end department stores to 7-Elevens. They customarily consist of anko sweet red bean paste wrapped in a thin layer of mochi dough, but these days, you'll find all sorts of interesting variations. My favorite store-bought daifuku variation is to swap the red bean paste for a plump, chocolate-covered strawberry.

MAKES 18 DUMPLINGS

- 1 cup / 204 g mochiko
- 1/4 cup / 50 g sugar
- Cornstarch, for dusting
- About 1 cup / 237 g azuki sweet red bean paste

1. In a medium bowl, combine the mochiko and 2/3 cup / 160 ml water and knead the dough with your hands until smooth. Stir in the sugar. The dough should have a porridge-like consistency.

2. In a medium nonstick pan set over medium heat, cook the mochi dough; stir constantly using a rubber spatula. Cook until the mochi becomes very thick, slightly translucent, and hangs together as a dough, about 5 minutes. Remove the mochi to the bowl, sprinkle the surface generously with cornstarch, and cover with plastic wrap. Place in the refrigerator for 30 minutes to chill.

3. Dust a cutting board heavily with cornstarch and prepare a baking sheet by lining it with parchment paper. With cornstarch-dusted fingers, pinch off a generous tablespoon of chilled mochi—it will be very sticky—and place it on the cutting board. Using a rolling pin coated in cornstarch, roll the mochi into a 3-inch / 7.5 cm round about 1/8-inch / .3 cm thick. Place the finished mochi wrapper on the baking sheet and roll the remaining wrappers.

4. One at a time, fill each mochi wrapper with a tablespoon-sized ball of red bean paste, gathering up and pinching off the edges of the mochi to form a sealed ball. Place seam-side down and serve immediately, or store in a sealed container in the refrigerator for 1 day.

ゆず

YUZU

137	WINTER CITRUS TART
138	YUZU CHEESECAKE
141	NASHI PEAR CRUMBLE
143	JAPANESE CREAMSICLE ICE CREAM
144	YUZU BLUEBERRY POUND CAKE
147	YUZU VANILLA CUPCAKES
148	SPRING ANMITSU
151	BLACKBERRY YUZU SHERBET
152	PINEAPPLE YUZU SORBET

When it comes to growing and selling fruit, the Japanese are on a level all their own. Through meticulous farming practices and a commitment to seasonality, they manage to create some of the most spectacularly beautiful—and delicious—produce in the world.

In the springtime, the stores are filled with ruby red strawberries, bigger, sweeter, and juicier than anything I've tasted in America. In the summer, you'll find gorgeous cherries and oversized, tender white peaches called *momos*. Fruits are traditionally given as gifts, which has given rise to luxury fruit emporiums in Tokyo where the most exceptional, unblemished apples, grapes, strawberries, pears, and the like are beautifully packaged and sold for sky-high prices; here you're likely to find novelty square-shaped watermelons, or the famous, impeccably round Yubari cantaloupes which sell for as much as $500 per pair. Fruit isn't appreciated just as a food, but as a thing of great physical beauty.

Unfortunately, Food and Drug Administration (FDA) restrictions and long distances make it very difficult to import fresh Japanese-grown fruit here to the United States (trust me, we've tried: We went to great lengths to source those phenomenally fresh strawberries for Kyotofu's desserts, but ended up striking out). There is, however, one trademark Japanese fruit flavor that's readily available here in bottled juice form: yuzu.

YUZU

Yuzu is a citrus fruit native to China, but has been grown in Japan for over a thousand years. It's about the size and shape of a grapefruit with thick, knobbly yellow skin. The fruit comes into season in the winter months, and it's found almost exclusively in Japanese and Korean cuisine. The flesh and juice have a supremely tart, pungent taste reminiscent of both lemon and grapefruit, with a hint of floral notes. Yuzu contains three times as much vitamin C as a lemon, making it a great boost to the immune system during cold and flu season.

In Japanese cuisine, yuzu juice is traditionally used in savory dipping sauces. These days, you'll also find it featured in craft cocktails and desserts. At Kyotofu, I like to use it in sorbets, tarts, cookies, and cakes, as a more complex, exotic, and uniquely Japanese alternative to lemon. Whenever you use it, keep its potency in mind—a little bit goes a very long way.

本
KYOTOFU

winter citrus tart GF

Yuzu juice is very potent so when cooking with it, it's important to respect its limits and use it sparingly. Too much in a recipe can be overpowering and off-putting. For this citrus tart, I include just a small amount of yuzu juice with a much larger volume of comparatively mild lemon juice, but you'll be amazed at how the Japanese citrus fruit's signature taste shines through.

MAKES 1 9" or 23 cm TART

- 1½ cups / 188 g bread flour
- 1½ tablespoons cornstarch
- ⅓ cup / 38 g confectioners' sugar
- ¼ teaspoon salt
- 1 cup (2 sticks) / 227 g unsalted butter, divided
- 1 large egg
- 1¾ tablespoons powdered gelatin
- 1 cup / 198 g granulated sugar
- 11 large egg yolks
- ¾ cup / 180 ml lemon juice
- 1 tablespoon yuzu juice

1. For the tart crust: Place the flour, cornstarch, confectioners' sugar, and salt in the bowl of a food processor and pulse to combine. Divide 1 stick / 113 g of butter into 12 pieces, add it to the dry ingredients, and pulse until the mixture resembles a coarse meal, about 10 seconds. Add the egg and process until the mixture forms into a ball. Form the dough into a disk, wrap tightly in plastic wrap, and let chill for 30 minutes.

2. Preheat the oven to 350° F / 177°C. On a floured work surface, roll the dough out to ¼-inch / .5 cm thickness or press directly into a greased 9-inch / 23 cm tart pan. Cover with parchment paper filled with pie weights and bake it for 30 minutes. Remove from the oven and let cool to room temperature.

3. In a small bowl, sprinkle the gelatin over ¼ cup / 60 ml of cold water and let stand for 5 minutes to soften. In the bowl of an electric mixer fitted with a paddle attachment, cream the remaining 1 stick / 113 g of butter and beat in the granulated sugar. Add the egg yolks, one at a time, and then add the lemon juice, yuzu juice, and bloomed gelatin powder. Mix until well combined.

4. Transfer the lemon curd to a medium saucepan over low heat and cook to just below a simmer, stirring constantly with a wooden spoon until thickened, about 10 minutes. Remove the pan from the heat and let the mixture cool slightly.

5. Transfer the lemon curd to the tart shell and refrigerate until set, at least 2 hours. Serve chilled or at room temperature.

yuzu cheesecake

This Japanese twist on lemon cheesecake uses yuzu's citrus tang to cut through the sweetness and density of cream cheese. For the lightest and fluffiest cheesecake, be sure that the creamed cheese has warmed to room temperature before you begin, and don't skimp on its time in the bowl of the electric mixer.

Serves 8 to 10

- 2 cups / 200 g graham cracker crumbs, from 14 to 16 crackers
- 3¾ teaspoons salt, divided
- ½ cup (1 stick) / 113 g unsalted butter, melted and cooled slightly
- 1 cup / 198 g granulated sugar
- 24 ounces / 680 g (3 packages) cream cheese, at room temperature
- 4 tablespoons yuzu juice
- 3 large eggs
- Shiro-An Cream (page 156)
- Black Sesame Tuile (page 167)

1. Preheat the oven to 350° F / 177°C. Wrap the bottom of a 9-inch / 23 cm springform pan in two layers of aluminum foil, to prevent water from leaking in at the seams.

2. In the bowl of a food processor, process the graham crackers into fine crumbs. In a medium bowl, combine the crumbs with ⅛ teaspoon salt and the melted butter and press the mixture into the bottom of a springform pan 9 to 10 inches / 23 to 25 cm in diameter. Bake for 10 minutes and let cool. Lower the oven temperature to 325° F / 163°C.

3. In the bowl of an electric mixer fitted with a paddle attachment, combine the sugar and cream cheese and mix on medium speed until light and fluffy, 3 to 5 minutes, scraping down the sides of the bowl at least once. Add the remaining salt and yuzu juice and mix until combined. Add the eggs one at a time, mixing until just combined. Pour the batter into the prepared crust.

4. Place the springform pan in a high-sided roasting pan and pour boiling water halfway up the sides of the springform pan. Bake for 90 minutes, then turn off the heat and leave the oven door cracked slightly for about 1 hour, allowing the cake to cool slowly to prevent it from cracking. Chill the cake in the refrigerator for at least 4 hours. Serves garnished with a dollop of Shiro-An Cream and a Black Sesame Tuile on each plate, if desired.

章 YUZU

頁 139

本
KYOTOFU

頁
140

nashi pear crumble gf

Crisp, sweet Nashi pears, which are often called Asian pears in the United States, taste and feel like a cross between an apple and a pear. Although they're most commonly eaten raw, I like to toss them with yuzu juice and sugar and bake them into a crumble. Nashi pears have a tendency to become watery when cooked, but adding a little cornstarch to the mix works to thicken their juices to a saucy consistency.

SERVES 8

4 pounds / 1.8 kg Asian pears (about 4 pears), peeled, cored, and cut into ¾-inch / 2 cm chunks

½ cup / 99 g granulated sugar, divided

2 tablespoons cornstarch

2 tablespoons yuzu juice

1 tablespoon lemon zest

1 cup / 120 g all-purpose flour

½ cup / 109 g light brown sugar

¼ teaspoons salt

¼ teaspoon cinnamon

4½ ounces (1 1/8 sticks) / 128 g unsalted butter, chilled and cubed (plus more for greasing)

Japanese Creamsicle Ice Cream (page 143)

1. Preheat the oven to 375° F / 191°C. In a large bowl, mix together the pears, ¼ cup / 50 g sugar, cornstarch, yuzu juice, and lemon zest.

2. In the bowl of a food processor, combine the flour, brown sugar, remaining ¼ cup / 50 g granulated sugar, salt, and cinnamon and pulse until combined. Add the cubed butter and continue to pulse until the mixture begins to form together into small pebbles, about 30 seconds.

3. Prepare a 13 x 9-inch / 33 x 23 cm baking dish by greasing the bottom and sides with butter. Add the Asian pears and, using your fingers, distribute the crumble evenly across the top. Chill in the freezer for 5 minutes.

4. Bake for 55 to 60 minutes, or until the crumble topping is golden-brown and crisp and the Asian pears are bubbling. Remove the crumble from the oven and let cool for at least 30 minutes. Serve warm with a scoop of Japanese Creamsicle Ice Cream, if desired.

CELEBRATING THE SEASONS

Seasonality is something of a buzzword in America these days, with restaurants taking great pains to demonstrate that their kitchens and menus move with rhythms of local agriculture.

But the concept of eating with the seasons has always been a big part of Japanese foodways. It can be summed up in the word *kisetsukan*: "a sense of the seasons." *Kisetsukan* isn't just a way of eating but a way of living, a fundamental part of the Japanese psyche. Shinto, the indigenous religion of Japan, orients itself around the worship of nature and attention to its changing beauty. Seasonal festivals celebrating occasions like harvest, rice planting, and the flowering of the cherry blossoms have long been central to Japanese culture, and continue to be to this day.

The Japanese have a word to describe foods at their seasonal perfection: *shun*, the exact moment when a fruit or vegetable is at its very best. Certain foods are not only associated with one season or another based on when they reach *shun*, but become symbolic of that season, and eating them a way of honoring and celebrating nature. Matsutake mushrooms, sweet potatoes, and chestnuts are all autumn signatures; yuzu, pickled turnip, and persimmon dominate winter; strawberries, bamboo shoots, and *sansai*, or foraged "mountain vegetables" conjure spring; summer's enormous *momo* peaches, cherries, and eggplant mark the transition into the warmest weather. Seafood has seasonality to it, too: the availability of various fish species changes with the calendar.

The concept of seasonality extends beyond the meal itself to tableware and decor. Autumn and winter call for warm, deep earthenware and pottery vessels, whereas in warm months food is typically served on light, flat dishware painted in bright colors. Glass, which has the appearance of ice, is favored during summer.

The flavors and shapes of *wagashi* shift to match the seasons, and desserts as a whole are influenced by the seasonality of different fruit flavors. Think about baking with Nashi pears and apples in the fall, passion fruit, yuzu, and persimmon in the winter, berries of all kinds in the spring, and peaches in the summer months.

japanese creamsicle ice cream

The marriage of citrus and vanilla is a time-tested ice cream favorite. Here, a splash of yuzu replaces orange juice to add a tart new dimension to the classic creamsicle concept.

MAKES 3 CUPS or 710 ml

1 cup / 235 ml heavy whipping cream

1½ cups / 355 ml whole milk

½ cup / 99 g granulated sugar

¼ teaspoon salt

½ vanilla bean

4 large egg yolks

¾ teaspoon vanilla paste or vanilla extract

1 tablespoon yuzu juice

1. In a small saucepan over medium heat, bring the cream, milk, sugar, and salt to a simmer, about 5 minutes. Split the vanilla bean open lengthwise and scrape its seeds into the milk mixture, whisking briskly to distribute them; add the bean to the pan. Cover, remove from the heat, and let infuse for 1 hour.

2. Fill a large bowl with ice water and set it aside. Remove the vanilla bean. In a separate bowl, whisk together the egg yolks and vanilla paste. Whisking constantly, gradually pour about half of the milk mixture into the yolk mixture. Stir the warmed yolk mixture back into the saucepan and cook over medium heat, stirring constantly with a wooden spoon or heat-resistant spatula until the custard thickens enough to coat the back of a spoon, about 5 minutes.

3. Strain the custard using a fine mesh sieve into a medium heat-resistant bowl set in the ice bath; stir frequently until the custard cools to room temperature. Stir in the yuzu juice. Cover the bowl with plastic wrap and chill thoroughly in the refrigerator.

4. Freeze the custard in an ice cream machine according to the manufacturer's instructions.

yuzu blueberry pound cake gf

This is pound cake done the Japanese way: light as air, subtly flavored, and gently sweet. You'll get the tenderest results if you let the butter, eggs, and sour cream warm to room temperature before use. Cold ingredients can mean a denser finished product.

MAKES 1 9" x 5" or 23 x 13 cm LOAF

- ½ cup (1 stick) / 113 g unsalted butter, softened
- ⅔ cup / 135 g granulated sugar
- 2 large eggs, at room temperature
- 1½ tablespoons lemon zest, from one lemon
- 1 tablespoon yuzu juice
- ¼ cup / 57 g sour cream, at room temperature
- 2 tablespoons vegetable oil
- 1¼ cups / 150 g all-purpose flour
- 1½ teaspoons baking powder
- ¾ teaspoon salt
- 1½ cups / 255 g fresh or frozen blueberries

1. Preheat the oven to 350° F / 177°C. Grease and flour a 9 x 5-inch / 23 x 13 cm loaf pan.

2. In the bowl of an electric mixer fitted with a paddle attachment, cream together the butter and sugar until light and fluffy, about 5 minutes. With the mixer running on medium speed, add the eggs one at a time, followed by the lemon zest. Add the yuzu juice, sour cream, and vegetable oil, and mix until well combined.

3. In a medium bowl, sift together the flour, baking powder, and salt. Add the dry ingredients to the bowl of the electric mixer and mix until just combined, scraping down the sides of the bowl at least once. Stir in the blueberries by hand.

4. Scrape the batter into the loaf pan, smoothing its surface with a spatula. Bake for 45 minutes, or until a cake tester comes out clean.

章 YUZU

本
KYOTOFU

yuzu vanilla cupcakes gf

The cupcake craze only recently hit Japan, and today these single-serving sweets are still relatively hard to find most places outside of Tokyo. Still, I loved the idea of flavoring this signature American treat with yuzu for a twist on lemon cake. Vanilla rounds out its citrus sharpness. We don't frost these cupcakes, which keeps them from getting too sweet, instead opting to top them simply with almonds for a little bit of crunch.

MAKES 12 CUPCAKES

- 9 ounces / 255 g white chocolate, chopped
- ½ cup (1 stick) / 113 g unsalted butter
- ⅓ cup / 80 ml soy milk
- ½ cup / 120 ml yuzu juice
- 1½ cups / 180 g all-purpose flour
- 1½ teaspoons baking powder
- ½ teaspoon salt
- ¾ cup / 86 g confectioners' sugar
- 4 large eggs, at room temperature
- 1 tablespoon vanilla extract
- ½ cup / 57 g slivered almonds, for topping

1. Preheat the oven to 350° F / 177°C. Prepare a cupcake tin by lining the molds with paper liners.

2. In a double boiler set over simmering water, heat the white chocolate, butter, soy milk, and yuzu juice until melted and combined. In a medium bowl, combine the flour, baking powder, and salt.

3. Pour the white chocolate mixture into the bowl of an electric mixer fitted with a paddle attachment. Add the confectioners' sugar immediately and whisk until the sugar is no longer visible. Add the eggs one at a time, followed by the vanilla extract. Gradually add the dry ingredients, mixing until just incorporated.

4. Fill each cupcake tin ⅔ to ¾ full with batter and sprinkle the slivered almonds over the top. Bake the cupcakes for 17 to 20 minutes, or until a toothpick or cake tester inserted comes out clean.

spring anmitsu

Anmitsu is the Japanese equivalent of an ice cream sundae: classic and unfussy, a tried-and-true ending to an evening meal. As familiar as it is to the Japanese, Western audiences can find the flavors and textures at play in anmitsu—jiggly, fruit-flavored agar squares, chewy shiratama dumplings, starchy azuki bean paste—well outside of their dessert comfort zones. Personally, I find it to be delicious; being that it's vegan and gluten free, it also suits a wide variety of guests and dietary restrictions. Try it at least once before forming an opinion!

SERVES 4

Blackberry Yuzu Sherbet (page 151)

Shiratama Dumplings (page 150)

1 cup / 260 g *yude* (chunky) azuki bean paste

Yuzu Agar (page 150)

¼ cup / 78 g Kuromitsu Syrup (page 169)

1. Place a generous scoop of Blackberry Yuzu Sherbet in four separate bowls. Add a Shiratama Dumpling and a ¼ cup / 65 g ball of azuki bean paste. Top each dessert with 1 cup Yuzu Agar cubes and drizzle a tablespoon of Kuromitsu Syrup over the top. Serve immediately.

章 YUZU

頁 149

yuzu agar

SERVES 4 to 6

3¾ teaspoons agar-agar

1 cup / 198 g sugar

½ cup / 120 ml yuzu juice

1. Prepare an 8 x 8-inch / 20 x 20 cm baking dish by lining it with plastic wrap. In a small saucepan over medium-high heat, boil the agar and 1¾ cups / 415 ml water until the mixture is clear. Reduce to a simmer. Whisk in the sugar and yuzu, stirring until well incorporated.

2. Pour the liquid into the baking dish and cover with plastic wrap. Refrigerate for at least 4 hours, or until gelled. Cut into ½- to ¾-inch / 1 to 2 cm cubes and reserve.

shiratama dumplings

MAKES 12 DUMPLINGS

1¼ cup / 180 g shiratamako

⅓ cup / 80 ml soy milk

1. Fill a medium-sized saucepan with water, cover, and bring to a boil. Meanwhile, fill a large bowl with ice and cold water and set aside.

2. In a medium bowl, combine the *shiratamako*, ⅓ cup / 80 ml water, and the soy milk, kneading the mixture with your hands until a tender dough forms. Form the dough into balls slightly smaller than a ping-pong ball, using your thumb to make a deep dimple or divot in the surface.

3. Add the dumplings to the boiling water and cook until they float to the surface, 3 to 4 minutes. Skim them from the boiling water and place them in an ice bath to cool.

blackberry yuzu sherbet

A sherbet, by definition, contains milk of some kind—typically, whole milk or cream. We use soy milk to keep this version vegan and dairy free while still giving it a little more body than a sorbet. Delicate yuzu juice doesn't stand up well to heat, so be sure to cool your sherbet base to around room temperature before adding it in for the best results.

MAKES 3 CUPS or 710 ml

- 2 cups / 475 ml soy milk
- 2/3 cup / 135 g granulated sugar
- 1/2 cup / 120 ml light corn syrup
- 1/2 cup / 123 g strained blackberry puree, from about 1 pint / 340 g blackberries
- 4 tablespoons yuzu juice

1. Fill a large bowl with ice and cold water and set aside. In a small saucepan set over medium heat, heat the soy milk, sugar, and corn syrup to a simmer.

2. Remove the pan from the heat, transfer the soy milk mixture to a heat-resistant bowl, and place it in the ice bath to chill. Once cooled to room temperature, stir in the blackberry puree and yuzu juice. Cover the bowl with plastic wrap and place in the refrigerator until fully chilled, at least 1 hour.

3. Freeze in an ice cream maker according to the manufacturer's instructions.

pineapple yuzu sorbet

This tart sorbet has a little bit of texture from the inclusion of pineapple pulp. If you prefer a perfectly smooth consistency, pass the pureed pineapple through a fine mesh sieve before adding it into the sorbet base; just be sure to start out with plenty of extra pineapple flesh, since much of the volume will be lost in straining.

Makes 1 pint or 475 ml

½ cup / 99 g granulated sugar

1 teaspoon light corn syrup

1⅓ cups / 301 g pureed pineapple flesh

4 tablespoons yuzu juice

1. Fill a large bowl with ice and cold water and set aside. In a saucepan set over medium-high heat, bring the sugar, corn syrup, and ½ cup / 120 ml water to a boil, swirling the pan until all the sugar is dissolved.

2. Remove the pan from the heat, transfer the sugar mixture to a heat-resistant bowl, and place it in the ice bath to chill. Stir in the pineapple flesh and yuzu juice. Once cooled to room temperature, cover the bowl with plastic wrap and place in the refrigerator until fully chilled, at least 1 hour.

3. Freeze in an ice cream maker according to the manufacturer's instructions.

基礎と伴奏

BASICS & ACCOMPANIMENTS

156	SHIRO-AN CREAM
157	SOY MASCARPONE CREAM
158	SAIKYO MISO CARAMEL SAUCE
159	PASSION FRUIT CRÈME ANGLAISE
160	CHOCOLATE-KINAKO SYRUP
161	POMEGRANATE YUZU SAUCE
162	SAFFRON CARAMEL SAUCE
163	SOY COCONUT CARAMEL
164	UME CARAMEL SAUCE
165	KURO CRÈME ANGLAISE
166	GINGER SYRUP
167	BLACK SESAME TUILE
168	MOMO MARSHMALLOWS
169	KUROMITSU SYRUP
170	COMICE PEAR AND SAKE SORBET
171	SOY CURD

shiro-an cream

Shiro-An, or white bean paste, is an arch-traditional Japanese dessert ingredient frequently found in wagashi (it's typically homemade, and very difficult to find in stores). This recipe combines it with whipped cream to create a silky dessert topper with a bit more body—and protein!—than whipped cream alone. I like to use a dollop to add a creamy touch and a little decoration to recipes like the Chocolate Tart (page 64), Warm Persimmon Mochi Chocolate Cake (page 62), and Winter Citrus Tart (page 137).

MAKES 1.5 CUPS or 355 ml

- 4 ounces / 113 g dried white navy beans
- ½ cup / 99 g granulated sugar
- ¾ cup / 180 ml heavy whipping cream
- ¾ teaspoon vanilla extract

1. Wash the beans in running water and then soak them, covered by at least 2 inches / 5 cm of cold water, overnight.

2. Drain the beans, transfer them to a medium saucepan, and cover generously with cold water. Bring the water to a boil over medium heat, reduce to a simmer, and let the beans cook for about 30 minutes, or until they are tender. Drain.

3. Puree the beans in a food processor or blender until smooth. Meanwhile in a medium saucepan over medium-high heat, combine the sugar with 2 tablespoons water and bring to a boil. Once the sugar has dissolved, reduce the heat to medium and add the bean paste in four to five additions, making sure to incorporate the syrup and bean paste well after each addition. Once the mixture is smooth, remove from the heat, strain through a fine mesh sieve, and let cool to room temperature. Measure out 1 cup / 340 g; reserve any remaining *shiro-an* for another use.

4. In the bowl of an electric mixer fitted with the whisk attachment, whip the heavy whipping cream and vanilla extract until soft peaks form. Add 1 cup / 340 g of *shiro-an* in several additions, continuing to whip until stiff peaks form and all the *shiro-an* is incorporated. Use immediately.

FOR A MATCHA VARIATION: Mix 1 tablespoon matcha powder into the *shiro-an* before adding it to the whipped cream.

FOR AN AZUKI VARIATION: Mix 45 grams (3 tablespoons) azuki bean paste into the *shiro-an* before adding it to the whipped cream.

soy mascarpone cream

A dollop of this creamy, nutty, lightly sweet whipped topping is a wonderful way to finish off tart or chocolaty recipes, such as the Jasmine Milk Chocolate Sweet Tofu (page 34) or Green Tea White Chocolate Cupcakes (page 83).

MAKES 1 CUP or 235 ml

½ cup / 170 g Soy Curd (page 171)

3 tablespoons mascarpone cheese

½ cup / 120 ml heavy whipping cream

1 tablespoon maple syrup

1. In a medium bowl, combine the Soy Curd and mascarpone, and whisk together well.

2. In a separate bowl, whip the heavy whipping cream to stiff peaks. Fold it into the soy mascarpone mixture, followed by the maple syrup. Use immediately.

saikyo miso caramel sauce

There's something absolutely magical as in the combination of miso and caramel, which together create a salty-sweet, buttery, luscious flavor that's simply unmatched by any other caramel sauce I've had. This sauce is totally addictive served over ice creams like Soy Milk (page 35), Chocolate Tofu (page 45), or Hojicha (page 79).

MAKES 2 CUPS or 475 ml

- ¾ cup / 149 g granulated sugar
- 1½ teaspoons light corn syrup
- ¼ cup (½ stick) / 57 g unsalted butter
- ½ cup / 120 ml heavy whipping cream
- ⅓ cup / 91 g saikyo miso
- ½ teaspoon salt

1. In a heavy-bottomed medium saucepan over medium-high heat, stir together the sugar, corn syrup, and 6 tablespoons of water to completely moisten the sugar. Heat, stirring constantly, until the sugar dissolves and the syrup begins to bubble. Stop stirring and allow the mixture to boil undisturbed until it turns a medium amber color. Immediately remove the caramel from the heat and whisk in the butter.

2. Slowly pour the heavy whipping cream into the caramel (it will bubble madly). Use a wooden spoon to stir the mixture until completely smooth. If any lumps remain, return the pan to the heat and stir until the lumps dissolve. Stir in the miso and salt and blend the mixture with a handheld electric mixer until smooth. Allow the sauce to cool slightly, then use immediately or store in the refrigerator for up to 1 week, heating before use.

passion fruit crème anglaise

A popular fruit flavor in Japanese desserts and confectionary, passion fruit adds a wonderful tropical tang to this creamy anglaise sauce. It can be spooned onto the plate beneath Maple Parfaits (page 41) to add a fruity dimension to that dessert; I also love the way it combines with matcha recipes, like the Green Tea Chocolate Cakes (page 78).

MAKES 1.25 CUPS or 295 ml

- ½ cup / 120 ml whole milk
- ½ cup / 120 ml heavy whipping cream
- ¼ cup / 50 g granulated sugar, divided
- 2 large egg yolks
- ¼ cup / 55 g passion fruit pulp, pureed and strained (from 5 small or 3 large fruits)
- ¾ tablespoon vanilla paste or vanilla extract

1. In a medium saucepan, combine the whole milk, heavy whipping cream, and 2 tablespoons of sugar and bring the mixture to a simmer, whisking until the sugar is dissolved.

2. Fill a large bowl with ice and cold water and set aside. In a medium bowl, whisk the egg yolks together with the remaining sugar and passion fruit puree.

3. Whisking constantly, gradually pour about half of the hot milk mixture into the yolk mixture. Stir the warmed yolks and milk back into the saucepan and cook over medium heat, stirring constantly with a wooden spoon or heat-resistant spatula until the custard thickens enough to coat the back of a spoon, about 5 minutes. Remove the pan from the heat and add the vanilla extract. Transfer the crème to the ice bath and let cool to room temperature. Use immediately, or store in the refrigerator for up to 3 days.

chocolate-kinako syrup

This quick, simple recipe uses kinako to add a little bit of earthy depth and a hint of peanut flavor to a standard chocolate syrup. It's at home on just about any ice cream, or drizzled on Black Sesame "Rare" Cheesecake (page 110).

MAKES 1.5 CUPS or 355 ml

½ cup / 120 ml heavy whipping cream

½ cup / 120 ml whole milk

4½ ounces / 128 g dark chocolate, chopped (64% cacao)

4 teaspoons kinako

1½ teaspoons vanilla bean paste or vanilla extract

1. In a small saucepan over medium heat, heat the heavy whipping cream and milk to just below a simmer, 3 to 5 minutes.

2. Remove the pan from the heat and add the chocolate, kinako, and vanilla paste. Cover and let sit for 2 minutes, and then whisk the sauce until smooth. Let cool slightly, and use immediately or store refrigerated for up to 1 week.

pomegranate yuzu sauce

A tart, fruit-forward sauce like this one works just wonderfully to balance out rich chocolaty or creamy desserts—think Black Sesame "Rare" Cheesecake (page 110) or Chocolate Tart (page 64). Taste the pomegranate and yuzu combination first before adding in the gelatin; if it's verging on too sour for your liking, you can adjust it with a little more sugar.

MAKES 1 CUP or 235 ml

- ½ teaspoon gelatin powder
- 1 cup / 235 ml unsweetened pomegranate juice
- 2 tablespoons granulated sugar
- 2 teaspoons yuzu juice

1. In a small bowl, sprinkle the gelatin over ¼ cup / 60 ml of cold water and let stand for 5 minutes to soften.

2. In a small saucepan set over medium heat, combine the pomegranate juice, sugar, and yuzu juice, and cook until the sugar is dissolved. Whisk in the gelatin, making sure to break up any lumps, and then remove the pan from the heat. Transfer the sauce to a heat-resistant container and let cool in the refrigerator until chilled, at least 1 hour, before serving.

saffron caramel sauce

Saffron is found throughout cuisines ranging from Spain to the Middle East to Asia. The precious, pricey red strands are also frequently encountered in Indian sweets, but their usage in traditional Japanese cuisine is fairly minimal—regardless, I couldn't resist the unique dimension that saffron lends to this caramel sauce.

MAKES 1 CUP or 235 ml

- 1 cup / 198 g granulated sugar
- ½ cup / 120 ml apple juice
- 1 ½ teaspoons cider vinegar
- 1 teaspoon saffron strands

1. In a heavy-bottomed medium saucepan set over medium-high heat, combine the sugar with 1 tablespoon water. Use a wet pastry brush to wash down any crystals from the side of the pan. Bring the mixture to a boil, gently swirling the pan to help dissolve the sugar. Let the solution boil without stirring; you will see the bubbles become fewer and larger. Once the color begins to change, watch your caramel very closely—it can go from undercooked to overcooked within a few seconds.

2. When the caramel reaches a light to medium amber color, remove it from the heat. Slowly pour in the apple juice and cider vinegar (the caramel will bubble madly). Use a wooden spoon to stir the mixture until completely smooth. If any lumps remain, return the pan to the heat and stir until they dissolve.

3. Add the saffron and let steep, covered, for 15 minutes. Strain the caramel through a fine mesh sieve and use immediately, or store in the refrigerator for up to 5 days and heat before use.

soy coconut caramel

This thick, rich caramel sauce is a perfect topper for ice cream flavors like Toasted Soy (page 51) or Sweet Miso (page 58). I also like to put it in a pastry bag or plastic squirt bottle and drizzle it over the top of Dark Chocolate Brownies (page 66) before serving.

MAKES 2 CUPS or 475 ml

- 1 cup / 198 g granulated sugar
- ¼ teaspoon lemon juice
- ⅓ cup / 80 ml soy milk
- ⅔ cup 160 ml coconut milk
- ¼ teaspoon salt

1. In a heavy-bottomed medium saucepan over medium-high heat, combine the sugar and lemon juice. Cook until the sugar begins to liquefy and darken at the edges; use a spatula or wooden spoon to drag the liquid sugar towards the center of the pan, keeping any brown spots from burning. Watch the pan carefully; lower the heat if the caramel darkens too quickly before all of the sugar has liquefied.

2. Once the caramel reaches a medium brown color, about 5 minutes, remove the pan from the heat and add the soy milk and coconut milk in a slow, steady stream, whisking constantly (the caramel will spit and seize). Whisk in the salt. Return the pan to the heat and continue to whisk until the caramel is smooth. Remove the caramel from the heat and let cool slightly. Use immediately or store in the refrigerator; microwave to warm before use.

ume caramel sauce

Astringent ume plums are a fruit particular to Japan. They can't be eaten raw, but are pickled into a popular treat called umeboshi or mixed with sugar and alcohol to make umeshu, or plum wine. Umeshu cuts the richness of this caramel sauce with its unique tart, fruity flavor.

MAKES 1.5 CUPS or 355 ml

1¼ cups / 248 g granulated sugar

⅔ cup / 160 ml umeshu plum wine

1. In a heavy-bottomed medium saucepan over medium-high heat, stir together the sugar with ¾ cups / 180 ml water. Heat, stirring constantly, until the sugar dissolves and the syrup begins to bubble. Stop stirring completely and allow the mixture to boil undisturbed until it turns a medium amber color.

2. Immediately remove the caramel from the heat and slowly pour the *umeshu* into the caramel (it will bubble madly). Use a wooden spoon to stir the mixture until completely smooth. If any lumps remain, return the pan to the heat and stir until dissolved. Use immediately or store in the refrigerator for up to 1 week, heating before use.

kuro crème anglaise

This cream sauce combines the bold, molasses taste of Japanese black sugar—kurosato—with vanilla and soy for a gorgeously rich, rounded flavor profile.

MAKES 2 CUPS or 475 ml

- ⅓ cup / 66 g granulated sugar
- ½ vanilla bean
- ⅔ cup / 160 ml whole milk
- ⅔ cup / 160 ml soy milk
- ⅓ cup / 67 g kurosato tiles
- 2 large egg yolks
- ¼ teaspoon vanilla extract

1. Pour the sugar into a small bowl. Slice open the vanilla bean lengthwise and scrape the seeds into the sugar, add the bean. Rub the sugar and vanilla seeds between your fingers until the seeds are evenly distributed.

2. In a medium saucepan, combine the milk, soy milk, *kurosato*, and vanilla sugar, and bring the mixture to a simmer, whisking until all of the sugar is dissolved.

3. Fill a large bowl with ice and cold water and set aside. In a small bowl, whisk the egg yolks together. Whisking constantly, gradually pour about half of the hot milk mixture into the yolk mixture. Stir the warmed yolks and milk back into the saucepan and cook over medium heat, stirring constantly with a wooden spoon or heat-resistant spatula until the custard thickens enough to coat the back of a spoon, about 5 minutes. Remove the pan from the heat and add the vanilla extract. Discard the spent vanilla bean. Transfer the crème anglaise to a heat-resistant bowl in the ice bath and let cool to room temperature. Use immediately, or store in the refrigerator for up to 3 days.

ginger syrup

We first used this simple ginger syrup as an accompaniment for the Ginger "Okayu" Rice Pudding (page 125), to punch up the dessert's ginger flavor. It's also excellent drizzled over ice cream, Soy Milk (page 35), or Kinako Waffles (page 42).

MAKES 1 CUP or 235 ml

1 cup / 198 g granulated sugar

4-inch / 10 cm knob fresh ginger, peeled and thinly sliced

1. In a medium saucepan set over medium heat, combine the sugar, 1 cup / 235 ml water, and ginger, and bring to a simmer. Simmer uncovered for 15 minutes.

2. Remove the pan from the heat, cover, and let steep for 45 minutes to an hour. Strain through a fine mesh sieve, discarding the ginger and reserving the syrup.

black sesame tuile

Tuiles are beautifully thin, crispy, delicate cookies that we like to use in desserts like cheesecakes, mousses, or puddings for a bit of extra crunch and a pretty garnish. They can be made in a wide range of shapes and sizes; search online or at a baking supply store for tuile templates, or make your own stencils at home by cutting shapes out of plastic or heavy paper. If you decide to make tuiles much larger than the ones described here, adjust the baking time accordingly.

MAKES 24 COOKIES

1¼ cups / 248 g granulated sugar

½ cup / 60 g all-purpose flour

1 cup / 142 g toasted black sesame seeds, ground to a fine flour in a spice grinder

½ cup / 120 ml orange juice

1 teaspoon yuzu juice

1 teaspoon lemon juice

1½ tablespoons black sesame paste

¼ cup (½ stick) / 57 g unsalted butter, melted

1. Preheat the oven to 350° F / 177°C. In the bowl of an electric mixer fitted with a paddle attachment, combine the sugar, flour, sesame flour, orange juice, yuzu juice, lemon juice, and black sesame paste, and mix to combine. Add the melted butter and mix until well combined.

2. Line a baking sheet with a nonstick baking mat or parchment paper. Lay down a stencil full of 3 x 1-inch / 7.5 x 2.5 cm rectangles and, using a bench scraper or another straight edge, spread the dough ⅛-inch / .3 cm thick over the top. Remove the stencil and scrape the excess dough back into the bowl.

3. Bake the cookies for 3 minutes, rotate the pan halfway, and bake for 2 minutes more, or until crisp throughout. Remove from the oven and let cool. Repeat until all the batter has been used. Store the cookies in the refrigerator in an airtight container for up to 1 week.

FOR A WHITE SESAME VARIATION: Replace the black sesame seeds and black sesame paste with equal volumes of white sesame seeds and white sesame paste.

momo marshmallows

Store-bought marshmallows have nothing on the soft, silky versions that you can make in your own kitchen. Momos are Japanese white peaches, those large, incredibly juicy fruits that double as a favorite candy flavor across Japan. While you can't get true Japanese momos in the United States, our domestic white peaches work just fine for this recipe. Eat these marshmallows on their own, or serve them along with Green Tea Yokan (page 90), Miso Mochi (page 122), and Brown Rice "Nama" Chocolates (page 126) for a delightful spread of miniature desserts.

MAKES 16 2" MARSHMELLOWS

- 2 very ripe white peaches, peeled and pitted
- 4 teaspoons powdered gelatin
- 2¼ cups / 447 g granulated sugar
- ½ cup / 120 ml plus 2 tablespoons light corn syrup
- ¼ teaspoon salt
- 3 large egg whites
- Confectioners' sugar, for dusting
- Cornstarch, for dusting

1. Puree the peaches in a blender or food processor until smooth. Pass the puree through a fine mesh sieve, reserving ⅔ cup / 160 ml of flesh and saving the rest for another use.

2. In a small bowl, sprinkle the gelatin over ¼ cup / 60 ml of cold water and let stand for 5 minutes to soften. Strain out the water and place the gelatin in the bowl of an electric mixer fitted with a whisk attachment.

3. In a saucepan fitted with a candy thermometer over medium-high heat, combine the sugar, corn syrup, salt, and peach puree. Cook, swirling the pan from time to time, until the thermometer reaches 240° F / 116°C or it can be formed into a soft ball in cold water, 7 to 10 minutes.

4. With the mixer running on low speed, immediately pour the peach mixture over the gelatin. Whisk the mixture on high speed until it becomes very thick, opaque, and has tripled in size, 5 to 7 minutes.

5. In a separate bowl, beat the egg whites until stiff peaks form. Add the whites into the sugar mixture and beat just until combined.

6. Line an 8-inch square pan with plastic wrap, spray with a nonstick cooking spray, and dust generously with powdered sugar and cornstarch. Pour the marshmallow batter into the pan, spreading and smoothing using a lightly-oiled spatula. Dust the surface with more powdered sugar and cornstarch and chill in the refrigerator, uncovered, for at least 3 hours.

7. Invert the marshmallow onto a cutting board and cut into 2-inch / 5 cm cubes. Roll each cube in confectioners' sugar and store in an airtight container at room temperature for up to 1 week.

kuromitsu syrup

The name of this sugar syrup translates from the Japanese as "black honey," but think of it as the Japanese answer to molasses. It's a popular and traditional dessert flavor in Japan, wonderful to drizzle anything from Sweet Tofu Pudding (page 32) to Kinako Waffles (page 42), Dorayaki Pancakes (page 47), or your morning yogurt.

MAKES 1 GENEROUS CUP or 235 ml

1 heaping cup / 67 g kurosato tiles

½ cup / 99 g granulated sugar

1. In a medium saucepan set over medium heat, stir together 1 cup / 235 ml of water with the *kurosato* tiles and granulated sugar. Bring the mixture to a simmer, breaking up the tiles with the back of a spoon and stirring regularly. Once the mixture has reached a simmer, about 5 minutes, reduce the heat to low and let simmer gently for 5 to 10 minutes, stirring from time to time until the syrup has thickened just to about the consistency of maple syrup.

2. Remove the syrup from the heat and let cool to room temperature. Use immediately or store in the refrigerator for up to 2 weeks.

comice pear and sake sorbet

This super easy recipe—just one step!—makes for an elegant summer dessert. Use nigori sake if you can find it; the unfiltered, cloudy style of rice wine adds wonderful natural body to the sorbet.

MAKES 3 CUPS or 710 ml

2 cups / 326 g Comice pears, peeled and diced (about 2 medium pears)

½ cup / 99 g granulated sugar

1 cup / 235 ml sake, preferably the nigori variety

1 tablespoon lemon juice

1. Combine the pears, sugar, and half of the sake in a blender or the bowl of a food processor and process the mixture until smooth. Add the lemon juice and the rest of the sake and blend for 15 to 30 seconds more. Freeze in an ice cream maker according to the manufacturer's instructions.

soy curd

This soy milk pastry cream is used in this book as a component in Soy Mascarpone Cream (page 157). It can also be put to good use as a filling for doughnuts, tarts, or layers cakes.

MAKES 1.5 CUPS or 355 ml

- 1 1/3 cups / 315 ml soy milk
- 1/4 cup / 50 g granulated sugar, divided
- 4 large egg yolks
- 1/4 cup / 30 g all-purpose flour
- 1/4 teaspoon vanilla extract

1. In a medium saucepan over medium heat, combine the soy milk and 2 tablespoons of the sugar, and bring the mixture to a simmer, about 5 minutes.

2. In a separate bowl, whisk together the egg yolks, flour, and the remaining sugar.

3. Fill a large bowl with ice and cold water and set aside. Whisking constantly, gradually pour about half of the hot milk mixture into the yolk mixture. Stir the warmed yolks and milk back into the saucepan and cook over medium heat, stirring constantly with a wooden spoon or heat-resistant spatula until the curd thickens enough to coat the back of a spoon, about 5 minutes (do not allow the mixture to boil). Remove the pan from the heat and add the vanilla extract.

4. Transfer the Soy Curd to a heat-resistant bowl in the ice bath and let cool to room temperature. Use immediately, or store in the refrigerator for up to 3 days.

ACKNOWLEDGMENTS

There are so many people who have helped bring Kyotofu and this cookbook to life.

First and foremost, I would like to thank my family for always believing in me and what I am trying to achieve—be it a restaurant, Japanese dessert brand, or kitchen incubator. Kyotofu would not be here without you. Life is nothing without my family. I love you Mom, Dad, Dani, Grandma, Pop-pop, Annie, and Riley.

I would also like to thank my business partner, Chef Michael Hu, for helping me refocus the brand during a very difficult time. I have learned much from you. You are absolutely vital to both Kyotofu's and my personal success.

To my pastry chefs and loyal staff over the years—including Michelle Park, Pauline Balboa, Inky Pak, Karina Strobl, Pedro Arvizu, and countless other sous chefs, pastry cooks, waitstaff, and packing staff—I greatly appreciate all of your hard work, input and inspirations, and belief in Kyotofu.

To my co-author, Liz Gunnison Dunn, who made this book what it is.

To my incredible agent, Sharon Bowers, thank you for believing and in me and in this book even when I was skeptical. I am grateful to have met and worked with you.

To Susan Van Horn, Zac Leibman, and everyone at Running Press—thank you for bringing this book to life!

index

A
agar-agar, defined, 20
azuki bean paste, defined, 20
azuki variation on Shiro-An Cream, 156

B
blackberries
    Blackberry Yuzu Sherbet, 151
    Spring Anmitsu, 148
Blackberry Yuzu Sherbet, 151
Black Sesame Caramel Mousse, 103
Black Sesame and Chocolate Mousse
    Tartlets, 107
Black Sesame Filling, 115
Black Sesame Macarons, 113
Black Sesame "Rare" Cheesecake, 110
Black Sesame Shortbread, 100
Black Sesame Tuile, 167
blueberries
    Yuzu Blueberry Pound Cake, 144
Brownies, Dark Chocolate, 66
Brown Rice Financiers, 120
Brown Rice Madeleines, 119
Brown Rice "Nama" Chocolates, 126

C
cake
    Green Tea Cake with Ginger Mousse, 38
    Hoji Roll Cake, 93
    White Sesame Cake, 99
    Yuzu Blueberry Pound Cake, 144
candies
    Brown Rice "Nama" Chocolates, 126
    Daifuku, 131
    Green Tea Yokan, 90
    Miso Mochi, 122
    Momo Marshmallows, 168
caramel
    Black Sesame Caramel Mousse, 103
    Caramel, 104
    Chocolate Tofu Ice Cream with Ume
        Caramel Sauce, 45
    Saffron Caramel Sauce, 162
    Saikyo Miso Caramel Sauce, 158
    Soy Coconut Caramel, 163
    Sweet Miso Ice Cream with Saffron
        Caramel Sauce, 58
    Ume Caramel Sauce, 83
celebrating the seasons in Japanese
    cooking, 142
chai variation on Dark Chocolate
    Brownies, 66
cheesecake
    Black Sesame "Rare" Cheesecake, 110
    Matcha "Rare" Cheesecake, 84
    Raspberry Cheesecake, 61
    Yuzu Cheesecake, 138
Chestnut Mousse, 50
Chinese Five-Spice Cream, 44
chocolate
    Black Sesame and Chocolate Mousse
        Tartlets, 107
    Brown Rice "Nama" Chocolates, 126
    Chocolate Chunk Cookies, 37
    Chocolate Glaze, 109
    Chocolate-Kinako Sauce, 160
    Chocolate Mousse, 108
    Chocolate Soufflé Cupcakes with
        Shiro-An Cream, 56
    Chocolate Tart, 64
    Chocolate Tofu Ice Cream with Ume
        Caramel Sauce, 45
    Dark Chocolate Brownies, 66
    Green Tea Chocolate Cakes, 78
    Green Tea White Chocolate
        Cupcakes, 83
    Jasmine Milk Chocolate Sweet Tofu, 34
    Milk Chocolate Mousse, 108
    Warm Persimmon Mochi Chocolate
        Cake, 62
Chocolate Chunk Cookies, 37
Chocolate Glaze, 109
Chocolate-Kinako Syrup, 160
Chocolate Mousse, 108
Chocolate Soufflé Cupcakes with
    Shiro-An Cream, 56
Chocolate Tart, 64
Chocolate Tofu Ice Cream with Ume
    Caramel Sauce, 45
citrus. See also yuzu
    Winter Citrus Tart, 137
coconut
    Soy Coconut Caramel sauce, 163
cookies and bars
    Black Sesame and Chocolate Mousse
        Tartlets, 107
    Black Sesame Macarons, 113
    Black Sesame Shortbread, 100
    Black Sesame Tuile, 167
    Brown Rice Financiers, 120
    Brown Rice Madeleines, 119
    Chocolate Chunk Cookies, 37
    Dark Chocolate Brownies, 66
    Soy Gingerbread Men, 38
    White Sesame Biscotti, 97
Comice Pear and Sake Sorbet, 170
Crème Brûlée, Matcha, 37
cupcakes
    Chocolate Soufflé Cupcakes with
        Shiro-An Cream, 56
    Green Tea Chocolate Cakes, 78
    Green Tea White Chocolate
        Cupcakes, 83
    Japanese Mont Blancs, 48
    Warm Persimmon Mochi Chocolate
        Cake, 62
    Yuzu Vanilla Cupcakes, 147

D-E
Daifuku, 131
dairy-free sweets
    Blackberry Yuzu Sherbet, 151
    Chocolate Tofu Ice Cream with Ume
        Caramel Sauce, 45

Comice Pear and Sake Sorbet, 170
Daifuku, *131*
Green Tea Yokan, *90*
Miso Mochi, *122*
Momo Marshmallows, *168*
Pineapple Yuzu Sorbet, *152*
Dark Chocolate Brownies, 66
Dorayaki Pancakes, *47*

F

feeding beautiful skin (through the Japanese diet), 59
fillings
Black Sesame Filling, 115
Ginger Mousse, 75
Milk Chocolate Mousse, 108
Persimmon Mochi, 63
Soy Curd, 171
flour, gluten-free, 27
fruit, a word about Japanese, 134–35.
For recipes, see *individual fruit listings*

G

genmai variation on Black Sesame Shortbread, *100*
ginger
Ginger Mousse, 75
Ginger "Okayu" Rice Pudding, *125*
Ginger Syrup, 166
Soy Gingerbread Men, 38
variation on Matcha Crème Brûlée, *72*
Ginger Mousse, 75
Ginger "Okayu" Rice Pudding, *125*
gluten-free
Chocolate Tofu Ice Cream with Ume Caramel Sauce, 45
flour, 27
and vegan desserts, a note on, 26
green tea, an introduction to, 70–71.
(See **tea** *for specific types and recipes*)
Green Tea Cake with Ginger Mousse, 38
Green Tea Chocolate Cakes, 78
Green Tea Muffins, 87
Green Tea White Chocolate Cupcakes, *83*
Green Tea Yokan, *90*

H

hojicha. See **tea**
Hojicha Ice Cream, 79
Hoji Roll Cake, *93*

I

ice cream and sherbet
Blackberry Yuzu Sherbet, 151
Chocolate Tofu Ice Cream with Ume Caramel Sauce, 45
Comice Pear and Sake Sorbet, 170
Hojicha Ice Cream, 79
Japanese Creamsicle Ice Cream, 143
Matcha Ice Cream, 86
Passion Fruit Ice Cream, 129
Passion Fruit Mochi Ice Cream, 128
Pineapple Yuzu Sorbet, 152
Soy Milk Ice Cream with Chocolate-Kinako Syrup, 35
Spring Anmitsu, *148*
Sweet Miso Ice Cream with Saffron Caramel Sauce, 58
Toasted Soy Ice Cream, 51
ingredients
photo of common Japanese, *23*
where to find Japanese, 25
iri genmai, defined, 20

J

Japanese
diet and beautiful skin, 59
ingredients, where to find, 25
pantry, stocking a, 20–24
tea, navigating the world of, 80–81
Japanese Creamsicle Ice Cream, 143
Japanese Mont Blancs, *48*
Japanese Toast, *76*
Jasmine Milk Chocolate Sweet Tofu, 34
jasmine tea, introduced, 20

K–L

kinako
defined, 21
Chocolate Chunk Cookies, 37
Chocolate-Kinako Sauce, 160
Japanese Mont Blancs, *48*
Kinako Waffles with Chinese Five-Spice Cream, *42*
Soy Gingerbread Men, 38
Kinako Waffles with Chinese Five-Spice Cream, *42*
Kuro Crème Anglaise, 165
kurumitsu
Ginger "Okayu" Rice Pudding, *125*
Kuromitsu Syrup, 169
Spring Anmitsu, *148*
Sweet Tofu Pudding with Kuromitsu Syrup, 32
Kuromitsu Syrup, 169
kurosato, defined, 21
Kyotofu
introduction to, 9–19
photos, *12–13*
Kyotofu Gluten-Free Flour, 27

M

Maple Parfait, *41*
matcha. See **tea**
Matcha Crème Brûlée, *72*
Matcha Ice Cream, 86
Matcha "Rare" Cheesecake, *84*
miso
Black Sesame "Rare" Cheesecake, *110*
Chocolate Soufflé Cupcakes with Shiro-an Cream, 56
Chocolate Tart, 64
Dark Chocolate Brownies, 66
defined, 21
Green Tea White Chocolate Cupcakes, 83
an introduction to, 50–51
Matcha "Rare" Cheesecake, *84*
Miso Mochi, 122
Raspberry Cheesecake, 61
Saikyo Miso Caramel Sauce, 158
Sweet Miso Ice Cream with Saffron Caramel Sauce, 58
Warm Persimmon Mochi Chocolate Cake, 62

Miso Mochi, 122
mochiko
    Daifuku, *131*
    defined, *21*
    Miso Mochi, *122*
Momo Marshmallows, *168*
Mont Blancs, Japanese, *48*
mousse
    Black Sesame Caramel Mousse, *103*
    Chestnut Mousse, *50*
    Ginger Mousse, *75*
    Milk Chocolate Mousse, *108*
muffins
    Green Tea Muffins, *87*

N–O

Nashi Pear Crumble, *141*
Nashi pears, defined, *21*

P–Q

Pancakes, Dorayaki, *47*
Parfait, Maple, *41*
passion fruit
    Maple Parfait, *41*
    Passion Fruit Crème Anglaise, *159*
    Passion Fruit Ice Cream, *129*
    Passion Fruit Mochi Ice Cream, *128*
Passion Fruit Crème Anglaise, *159*
Passion Fruit Ice Cream, *129*
Passion Fruit Mochi Ice Cream, *128*
pastries. *See* tarts
peaches
    Momo Marshmallows, *168*
pears
    Comice Pear and Sake Sorbet, *170*
    Nashi Pear Crumble, *141*
peppermint variation on Dark Chocolate Brownies, *66*
persimmon
    defined, *23*
    Persimmon Mochi, *63*
    variation on Ginger "Okayu" Rice Pudding, *125*
    Warm Persimmon Mochi Chocolate Cake, *62*

Persimmon Mochi, *63*
Pineapple Yuzu Sorbet, *152*
Pomegranate Yuzu Sauce, *161*
puddings and gelatins. *See also* mousse
    Ginger "Okayu" Rice Pudding, *125*
    Jasmine Milk Chocolate Sweet Tofu, *34*
    Matcha Crème Brûlée, *72*
    Sweet Tofu Pudding with Kuromitsu Syrup, *32*
    Yuzu Agar, *150*

R

Raspberry Cheesecake, *61*
rice (and rice flour)
    Brown Rice Financiers, *120*
    Brown Rice Madeleines, *119*
    Brown Rice "Nama" Chocolates, *126*
    Daifuku, *131*
    a few words about, *118*
    genmai variation on Black Sesame Shortbread, *100*
    Ginger "Okayu" Rice Pudding, *125*
    Miso Mochi, *122*
    Passion Fruit Mochi Ice Cream, *128*
    Persimmon Mochi, *63*
    Shiratama Dumpling, *150*

S

Saffron Caramel Sauce, *162*
Saikyo Miso Caramel Sauce, *158*
sake
    Comice Pear and Sake Sorbet, *170*
    defined, *23*
sauces
    Caramel, *104*
    Chocolate-Kinako Sauce, *160*
    Kuro Crème Anglaise, *165*
    Passion Fruit Crème Anglaise, *159*
    Pomegranate Yuzu Sauce, *161*
    Saffron Caramel Sauce, *162*
    Saikyo Miso Caramel Sauce, *158*
    Soy Coconut Caramel, *163*
    Ume Caramel Sauce, *164*

sesame desserts
    black, variation on Sweet Tofu Pudding, *32*
    Black Sesame Caramel Mousse, *103*
    Black Sesame and Chocolate Mousse Tartlets, *107*
    Black Sesame Filling, *115*
    Black Sesame Macarons, *113*
    Black Sesame "Rare" Cheesecake, *110*
    Black Sesame Shortbread, *100*
    Black Sesame Tuile, *167*
    seed paste, defined, *23*
    seeds
        defined, *23*
        an introduction to, *96*
    White Sesame Biscotti, *97*
    White Sesame Cake, *99*
Shiratama Dumpling, *150*
Shiro-An Cream, *156*
shiratamako, defined, *23. See also* rice / rice flour
Shortbread, Black Sesame, *100*
silken tofu
    Black Sesame "Rare" Cheesecake, *110*
    Chocolate Tofu Ice Cream with Ume Caramel Sauce, *45*
    defined, *24*
    Matcha "Rare" Cheesecake, *84*
    Toasted Soy Ice Cream, *51*
skin, the Japanese diet and, *59*
soy, an introduction to, *50–51*
soybean flour. *See* kinako
Soy Curd, *171*
Soy Gingerbread Men, *38*
Soy Mascarpone Cream, *157*
soy milk
    Blackberry Yuzu Sherbet, *151*
    defined, *24*
    Ginger "Okayu" Rice Pudding, *125*
    Japanese Toast, *76*
    Kuro Crème Anglaise, *165*
    making at home, *39*
    Matcha Crème Brûlée, *72*
    Soy Coconut Caramel sauce, *163*
    Soy Curd, *171*

Soy Milk Ice Cream with
    Chocolate-Kinako Syrup, 35
  Sweet Miso Ice Cream with Saffron
    Caramel Sauce, 58
Spring Anmitsu, *148*
stocking a Japanese pantry, 20–24
strawberries
  Japanese Toast, 76
sushi rice, defined, 24
syrups. *See also* **toppings**
  Ginger Syrup, 166
  Kuromitsu Syrup, 169
**Sweet Miso Ice Cream with Saffron
  Caramel Sauce,** *58*
**Sweet Tofu Pudding with Kuromitsu
  Syrup,** *32*

T

tarts
  Black Sesame and Chocolate Mousse
    Tartlets, 107
  Chocolate Tart, 64
  Winter Citrus Tart, 137
tea
  chai variation on Dark Chocolate
    Brownies, 66
  green, an introduction to, 70–71. See
    following entries hojicha; matcha
  hojicha
    defined, 20
    Hojicha Ice Cream, 79
    Hoji Roll Cake, 93
    variation on Black Sesame Short-
      bread, 100
    variation on Brown Rice "Nama"
      Chocolates, 126
  matcha
    defined, 21
    Green Tea Cake with Ginger
      Mousse, 38
    Green Tea Chocolate Cakes, 78
    Green Tea Muffins, 87
    Green Tea White Chocolate
      Cupcakes, 83
    Green Tea Yokan, 90
    Japanese Toast, 76
    Matcha Crème Brûlée, 72
    Matcha Ice Cream, 86
    Matcha "Rare" Cheesecake, 84
    Tokyo Tiramisu, 89
    variation on Black Sesame Filling, 115
    variation on Black Sesame
      Macarons, 114
    variation on Black Sesame
      Shortbread, 100
    variation on Brown Rice Financiers,
      120
    variation on Brown Rice "Nama"
      Chocolates, 126
    variation on Shiro-An Cream, 156
  navigating the world of Japanese,
    80–81
  the way of, 105
Tiramisu, Tokyo, *89*
Toasted Soy Ice Cream, *51*
tofu
  Chocolate Tofu Ice Cream with Ume
    Caramel Sauce, 23
  Jasmine Milk Chocolate Sweet Tofu, 34
  Matcha "Rare" Cheesecake, 84
  Sweet Tofu Pudding with Kuromitsu
    Syrup, 32
  Toasted Soy Ice Cream, 51
Tokyo Tiramisu, *89*
toppings. *See also* **sauces**
  Caramel, 104
  Chestnut Mousse, 50
  Chinese Five-Spice Cream, 44
  Chocolate Glaze, 109
  Ginger Syrup, 166
  Kuromitsu Syrup, 169
  Persimmon Mochi, 63
  Shiro-An Cream, 156
  Soy Mascarpone Cream, 157

U

Ume Caramel Sauce, *164*

V

**vegan desserts, a note on gluten-free
  and, 26**

W–X

**Waffles, Kinako, with Chinese Five-Spice
  Cream,** *42*
wagashi
  the art of, 123
  Dorayaki Pancakes, 47
  Green Tea Yokan, 90
  an introduction to, 12–13
**Warm Persimmon Mochi Chocolate
  Cake,** *62*
White Sesame Biscotti, *97*
White Sesame Cake, *99*
white sesame variation
  on Black Sesame Shortbread, 100
  on Black Sesame Tuile, 167
Winter Citrus Tart, *137*

Y–Z

yuzu
  Blackberry Yuzu Sherbet, 151
  an introduction to, 135
  Japanese Creamsicle Ice Cream, 143
  Nashi Pear Crumble, 141
  Pineapple Yuzu Sorbet, 152
  Pomegranate Yuzu Sauce, 161
  Spring Anmitsu, 148
  variation on Black Sesame Shortbread,
    100
  Winter Citrus Tart, 137
  Yuzu Agar, 150
  Yuzu Blueberry Pound Cake, 144
  Yuzu Cheesecake, 138
  Yuzu Vanilla Cupcakes, 147
Yuzu Agar, *150*
Yuzu Blueberry Pound Cake, *144*
Yuzu Cheesecake, *138*
yuzu juice, defined, 24
Yuzu Vanilla Cupcakes, *147*